QRP Notebook

by Doug DeMaw, W1FB

Published by the
AMERICAN RADIO RELAY LEAGUE
225 Main Street
Newington, CT 06111

Foreword

You *can* work the world with 5 watts or less. That's the philosophy of the QRP operator, along with "power is no substitute for operating skill." A contact halfway across the country with a 1-watt rig that *you* built can be just as rewarding as using a kilowatt to work a rare DX station halfway around the world.

Doug DeMaw, W1FB, has been writing articles about QRP operating and equipment construction for many years. In this book, Doub presents construction projects for the QRP operator, from a simple 1-watt crystal-controlled transmitter to more complex transceiver designs. Rather than simply presenting a collection of completed units, Doug guides you through the projects "building-block" style. This way, you gain an understanding of how the circuits operate and learn how the building blocks might be put together in other configurations.

Experimentation and low-power operating go hand in hand. Construction of a complete modern transceiver is a major undertaking, but some of the circuits in this book can be put together in an evening or a weekend from a few dollars' worth of parts. Once built, the equipment can be tested and improved as your understanding and skill grow. Many of the simpler circuits can be used later as parts of the more complex projects.

We hope that this book will encourage you to pick up the soldering iron and give one of the circuits a try. Experience firsthand the thrill of a contact with equipment *you* built.

David Sumner, K1ZZ
Executive Vice President

Newington, Connecticut
March 1986

Contents

PREFACE

QRP means something different to each of us. We may find our pleasure in operating at or below the recognized 5 watt maximum power level, and that may be where our primary interest ends. On the other hand, our maximum QRP pleasure may come from designing and building low-power transmitters and allied equipment. Some QRPers delight in both facets of the pastime. This booklet is dedicated primarily to the QRP builder, and there is minimum emphasis on the operating aspects of our unique hobby. A book that I consider excellent for first-time QRPers and those whose main interest is in operating was written by Adrian Weiss, WØRSP. The title is **The Joy of QRP.**

This book follows my preferred style of writing in plain language. You won't be distracted by needless formulas and deep technical explanations. We'll leave that for later research, should you be so disposed. The **ARRL Handbook** and **SOLID STATE DESIGN for the Radio Amateur** contain detailed explanations of how circuits function, along with the related mathematics. In this book we will consider proven practical QRP and related circuits. Guidelines are given for basic design activities, and we address also the typical ailments in QRP equipment, along with cures and some preventive procedures.

I will always maintain that the better part of Amateur Radio is found in the ham workshop. Any licensed operator can buy commercial gear and go on the air. But, the real thrill of QRP operation comes from build-your own equipment, innovating and experimenting. That was what radio was all about in the beginning, and those who have never experienced the joys of operating with homemade transmitters and receivers have missed the fulfillment that is due them.

Fancy diagrams and photographs are obtrusive by their absence. I chose a simple presentation format to keep the cover price of this book low. I hope you will have many of happy hours as you progress through these pages.

Vy 73, Doug DeMaw, W1FB/8 (ex W1CER, W8HHS)

QRP EQUIPMENT FORMAT

The question arises frequently about the best choice in equipment format -- transceivers versus separate transmitter and receiver. There are pros and cons for each lineup. The final decision rests with the QRP operator, and his or her style of operating will dictate the most convenient arrangement.

There is no question about small transceivers being the correct way to go when the equipment is to be used mainly as an emergency unit for such experiences as backpacking, hiking, boating, and such. A lightweight, self-contained CW package can be tucked into a small space, along with a simple antenna and a battery pack.

Conversely, the fixed-station operator can enjoy the luxury of an ac-operated dc power supply, separate transmitting and receiving packages, and a tad more dc-power input to the final stage of the transmitter.

Separate units enable the builder to modify one unit without taking the other piece (transmitter or receiver) out of service. We may frequently wish to improve the circuit of one of the mating units, or we may desire to replace it with a new circuit. Certainly, having "separates" is a convenience under these circumstances!

What other advantages are offered by using separate units? First, the need for RIT (receiver incremental tuning) is avoided. Also, we need not worry about the correct transmitter "frequency offset," as is the case when using a transceiver: We simply tune the receiver to the desired listening frequency.

Having separate equipment for transmitting and receiving does not imply that the composite QRP station needs to be large. To the contrary, many builders develop packages that are quite tiny. In fact, some "separates," combined, are much smaller than a number of transceivers I have seen . . . especially those made by commercial manufacturers.

For many of us the challenge of miniaturization is a motivating force when we design a new piece of QRP gear. W7ZOI and W7EL have demonstrated their craft quite well in this regard. Their work has appeared in **QST** (see Appendix).

I don't wish to sell transceivers short, by any means. They have their place, and are well suited for use with direct-conversion receivers, since a common LO frequency can be used for receiving and transmitting. The choice of format is yours.

SOME WORDS ABOUT ANTENNAS

The antenna is the lifeline of our QRP stations. The better the antenna performance the greater the distance we can span with our low-power signals. Ideally, we should add as many decibels as possible via the antenna system. This helps to compensate for the dBs we lose by operating with less than 5 watts. The QRP-station antenna should equal or exceed that of the QRO fixed station.

Despite this proven rule, a number of QRPers believe that the QRP-station antenna should also be modest and low cost. This is not a common-sense conclusion. Only a masochist would use an inferior antenna with a QRP rig!

What constitutes an inferior antenna? First, a random length of wire, close to the ground, might serve as an example. Yet, I've known a number of QRPers who were willing to settle for such a poor radiator. Secondly, partial-size antennas with traps or loading coils do not offer efficient performance. If you are running 100 watts, or a kW, you can afford to throw a few dB away by way of a compromise antenna: At the QRP level we should accept nothing short of first-rate antenna performance.

You may be asking at this juncture, "What is a good antenna?" A full-size dipole for the band of operation can be a good antenna if it is high above ground (1/2 wavelength or greater, in a best-case example), and when it is clear of nearby conductive objects, such as power lines, phone wires and other metal items that have reasonable mass. Of course, the feed line for the half-wave dipole should have minimum loss, and must be kept as short as practicable if we are to cut down the losses. Open-wire feeders offer the least loss.

Other good antennas are triband and single-band Yagis. Full-size vertical antennas with ground radials are also good. Some half-size verticals with proper top loading will do nicely for QRP work, assuming a decent ground system is used with the vertical radiator.

The **ARRL ANTENNA BOOK** describes all manner of good antennas, along with the principles that make them perform well. I recommend that book as a reference.

It is wise to keep in mind that dBs gained are cumulative in the overall system. Avoid lossy feed lines such as miniature RG-174/U. It is <u>very</u> lossy, as is some older surplus coaxial cable. Whenever possible, avoid the use of RG-58/U and opt for RG-8/U or even RG-8X.

2

CHAPTER 1

THE ESSENTIALS OF RECEIVING

It is important that the receiver in a QRP package be at least as good as the transmitter in terms of performance. This truism applies to any ham station, irrespective of the power class. What is meant by "as good as?" Generally, we perceive this to mean that   the receiver should be frequency-stable, it will exhibit good sensitivity, and will have ample overall gain (RF and audio sections combined) to provide adequate headphone or speaker volume for weak signals that are at or slightly above the noise threshold of the receiver.

What else should we look for in an adequate QRP receiver? High among the qualities is dynamic range. This means that the receiver must be able to accommodate large in-band or out-of-band signals without becoming desensitized or generating unwanted additional responses (IMD -- intermodulation distortion) within the RF amplifier and/or mixer stages. In the case of direct-conversion (DC) receivers, we must also guard against unwanted AM detection, common-mode hum and undue microphonics. All of the foregoing may seem like a large order when we sit down to design a receiver for our QRP adventures. True, some of the design criteria are difficult to realize, but it is possible to develop good receivers that are simple in design. In this chapter we will examine methods for avoiding pitfalls while achieving satisfactory performance.

For the most part, a receiver for use from 1.8 through 10.1 MHz should not require an RF amplifier ahead of the mixer or product detector to ensure an acceptable SNR (signal-to-noise ratio) if the first stage of the receiver is designed properly. At 14 MHz and above, a low-noise RF amplifier is recommended, since the receiver noise may exceed the noise coming in from the antenna (atmospheric and man-made noise).

The stability of the receiver local oscillator is important when a high order of selectivity of desired. In other words, the sharper the receiver filter is (IF or audio) the more pronounced the effects of oscillator drift. This consideration becomes highly significant if the QRP equipment is used for field work where the ambient temperature can change markedly from hour to hour. VXOs (variable crystal oscillator) offer an easy route to stability under severe environmental conditions.

1.1 Direct-Conversion Receivers

At this time the direct-conversion (DC) or synchrodyne receiver offers the utmost in design simplicity. In effect, a DC receiver is an advance in performance beyond the long-popular "genny" or regenerative receiver. The latter type was plagued by lack of "smoothness" in the feedback or regeneration control. Some settings caused dead spots, while others caused howling. Most of those receivers required resetting of the regeneration control as one tuned across a MHz or more of frequency range.

The DC receiver uses a separate oscillator to supply injection signal to the detector, whereas the regen receiver uses a detector that operates also as an oscillator -- hence the annoyance mentioned above.

A DC receiver consists of a tunable product detector that uses a variable beat-frequency oscillator (VBFO). This VBFO replaces the tunable local oscillator in superheterodyne receivers. The product detector in a DC receiver functions somewhat as the mixer in a superhet. So, the front end of a DC receiver can consist of a product detector and VBFO, unless an RF amplifier is used ahead of the detector.

Fig. 1-1 shows a block diagram of a typical DC receiver. Note the simplicity of the lineup.

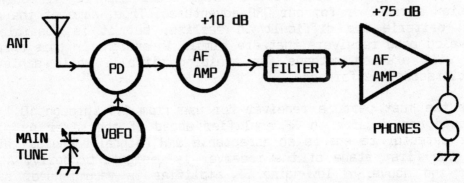

Fig. 1-1 -- Block diagram of a simple DC receiver.

Most of the receiver gain is developed in the audio section. This requires between 75 and 100 dB of audio gain to produce sufficient weak-signal output to the speaker or phones. Note also that the required selectivity for SSB or CW reception must be provided by means of audio filtering rather than RF filtering. Selectivity can be developed through the use of passive (inductors and capacitors) or active (transistors or ICs) audio filters that are located after the product detector. In order to enhance the noise figure of the audio channel, a low-noise AF amplifier should be included between the detector and the input of the audio filter, especially when active filters (noisy) are used.

1.2 DC Receiver Problems

Direct-conversion receivers suffer from hum and microphonics that do not normally show up in superhet receivers. The malady worsens as the operating frequency is increased. Many DC receivers become almost unusable at 14 MHz and above, especially when they are operated from an ac power supply. Why does this happen? First, the cause of microphonics (physical movement of electrical connections, such as tuning-capacitor bearings) is present in all types of receivers, but these RF disturbances are detected, converted to audio frequency, then greatly amplified by the high-gain audio channel in the DC receiver. These same noises might never be heard in a well-designed superhet.

Common-mode hum is the other plague of DC receivers. What causes this annoying hum? Why don't we hear it when using a battery power source? The problem is caused by VBFO energy entering the ac power supply via the dc and ac power leads, then reaching the rectifiers, where harmonics (clipped waves) of the VBFO are generated. This unwanted ac-modulated energy is radiated by the power-supply leads, picked up by the station antenna, then fed back into the product detector. It's a vicious circle!

There are cures for common-mode hum:

1) Install 0.01-uF bypass capacitors across the rectifier diodes (one for each diode).

2) Place a 0.01-uF capacitor from each side of the ac line (inside the power-supply cabinet) to chassis ground.

3) Wind a decoupling choke and install it near the power-supply dc output terminals. Use 25 turns of no. 22 wire (bifilar wound -- a pair of identical windings, side by side) on an Amidon FT114-61 ferrite toroid core (u_i = 125). The plus power-supply lead is thus passed through one choke wire, while the ground or negative lead is routed through the remaining choke wire.

4) Connect a good earth ground to the receiver chassis.

5) Do not use an end-fed wire antenna. Try to space the station antenna away from the shack and use coaxial-cable feed line.

I have found the foregoing preventive measures very effective in reducing or completely eliminating common-mode hum. The use of the bifilar-wound decoupling choke as a cure was initiated by W7ZOI some years ago.

1.3 The Product Detector

We are tempted frequently to relate circuit simplicity to the term "QRP." This, more often than not, can lead us down the path of trouble. For example, a typical "simple" product detector for a DC receiver might be a single dual-gate MOSFET (40673 or 3N211) or a single JFET, such as an MPF102 or 2N4416. Although detectors of this type (Fig. 1-2A) provide reasonable conversion gain (6 to 12 dB typically), the single-ended PD is subject to severe unwanted A-M detection. Strong A-M broadcast stations can overload the PD to create broadcast-station "blanketing" across all of a given amateur band. The circuit of Fig. 1-2A is recommended only for the simplest of portable or emergency gear, but not for all-round QRP operating, especially on the 40-meter band where countless loud BC stations are found.

The next-best approach to PD design for the front end of a DC receiver is the adoption of a singly balanced PD of the general type illustrated in Fig. 1-2B. Here we have two JFETs operating in a push-pull hookup, with the local oscillator (LO) fed to the JFETs in a parallel manner via the secondary center tap of T1. A toroidal tuned transformer (T1) is indicated. The antenna tap is located approximately 10% of the total primary turns above the grounded end of the winding. Although an equal number of turns may be used for the T1 secondary, it is common practice to use 0.25 or less the number of turns on the primary winding. This reduces the signal input to the PD, which aids the dynamic range (improved strong-signal performance). Best results will be had when the PD is laid out for symmetry of the electrical circuit. This will improve the balance. T2 is an audio interstage transformer (10K primary, 2K secondary).

Some ICs, such as the RCA CA3028A, serve nicely as singly balanced PDs, owing to the differential pair of bipolar transistors contained on the chip. Other ICs, such as the CA3046, also work well in this application. Examples are given in **Solid State Design** (ARRL). Similarly, we may use two matched bipolar transistors in place of the JFETs in Fig. 1-2B.

Our best results will be had when we use a doubly balanced PD at the front end of our DC receivers. The devices may be passive (diodes) or active (transistors or ICs). The greatest rejection of A-M signals will be enjoyed when using a doubly balanced PD. The classic diode-ring doubly balanced PD is seen in Fig. 1-2C. D1-D4, inclusive, should be matched for forward resistance. An ohmmeter is suitable for the purpose. Hot-carrier diodes are recommended, but high-speed switching diodes such as 1N914s are suitable when hot-carrier diodes are not available. Again, the layout of the detector should be symmetrical for best balance.

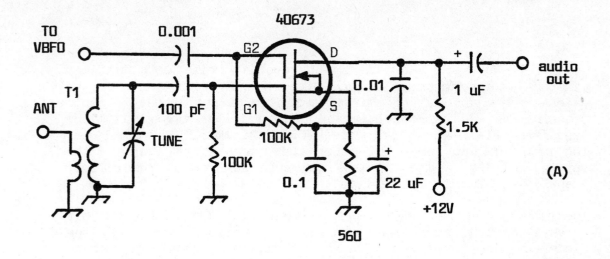

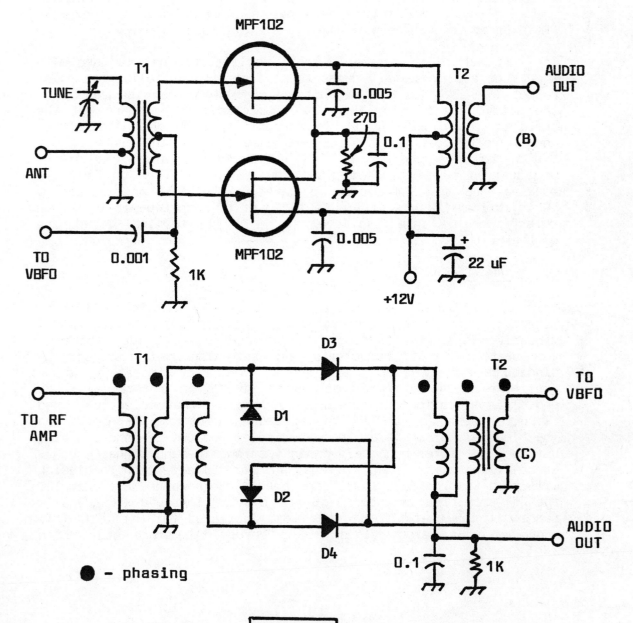

● − phasing

FIG. 1-2

T1 and T2 of Fig. 1-2C are small toroidal units with trifilar windings (three identical-length wires wound on the core at the same time -- parallel or twisted a few turns per inch). Suitable transformers can be made by winding 15 trifilar turns on Amidon Associates FT-37-43 ferrite cores (850 ui). No. 30 enameled wire can be used. The large dots over the transformers indicate the correct phasing of the windings. Be sure to hook up the circuit exactly as indicated by the dots.

The diode PD of Fig. 1-2C is a passive one. Rather than exhibit conversion gain, as do the circuits of A and B in Fig. 1-2, the diode-ring detector has a conversion loss. This means that approximately 8 dB of gain is lost in the DC receiver front end. This detector degrades the receiver NF (noise figure), which will lead to unacceptable weak-signal reception at 30 meters and higher. A low-noise RF amplifier should be used ahead of the diode-ring PD in order to provide gain and a workable noise figure.

The VBFO, which is a tunable local oscillator, that is used with the PD of a DC receiver, needs to deliver substantially more power output (+7 dBm) for the circuit of Fig. 1-2C than is needed for the active PDs of Fig. 1-2. The characteristic impedance at the ports of the diode-ring PD is approximately 50 ohms. Therefore, the LO voltage at T2 of Fig. 1-2C should be on the order of 0.5 V rms (as measured with a VTVM and RF probe), or 1.4 V pk-pk, as observed on a scope display. The two active PDs of Fig. 1-2 require roughly 6 V pk-pk at the gates of the FETs to allow proper LO injection. But, as little as 10 mW of LO output power is needed to achieve this injection level at the higher terminal impedances of the FET PDs.

1.4 RF Amplifiers

We may use bipolar transistors or FETs as receiver RF amplifiers. Both types of device can provide high gain and a low NF if treated properly. In an ideal design the RF amplifier provides not only the aforementioned characteristics, but also has good strong-signal capability (low IMD). Dynamic range is important to RF amplifiers, just as it is to mixers or PDs in a receiver front end. This situation can be aided by ensuring that selective tuned circuits are used at the input and output of the RF amplifier. The high selectivity aids in rejecting strong out-of-band signals, but does not offer much help against strong in-band signal energy. Generally, high operating voltages and careful attention to biasing will help to provide a low NF and good dynamic range. For example, the RF amplifier of Fig. 1-3B would have improved DR (dynamic range) if the operating voltage were increased to 18 or 20. This would allow a larger signal swing before the stage started to

RF AMPLIFIER

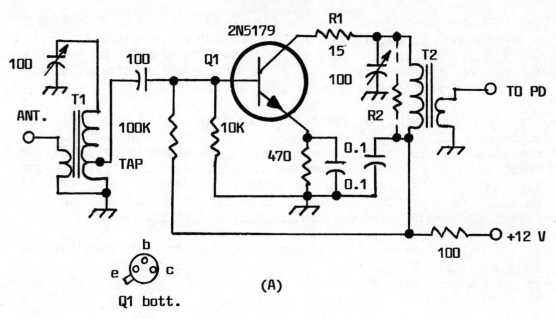

(A)

RF AMPLIFIER

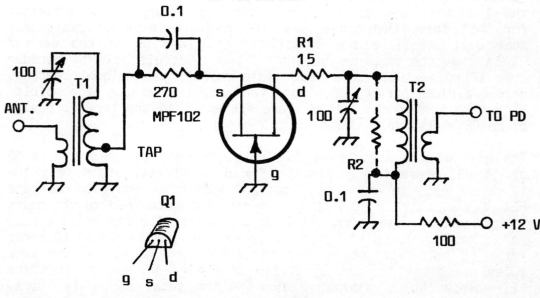

(B)

FIG. 1-3

overload. Two FETs in a series arrangement would permit even higher operating voltages to be used.

The CATV transistor indicated in Fig. 1-3A has a low NF and good high-frequency characteristics. Ft is 1200 MHz. Numerous VHF or UHF transistors can be used at Q1, assuming the NF is suitable for HF use. For the bands below 20 meters we may obtain satisfactory performance with the popular 2N2222A or 2N3904.

The tap point on T1 for the base of Q1 (Fig. 1-3A) is set at approximately 600 ohms. This location is found at 0.25 to 0.33 of the total turns. The T1 primary winding is approximately 10% the total secondary turns. T2 can be a duplication of T1, minus the tap. Amidon T50-2 (red) toroid cores are suitable for T1 and T2 up to 20 meters. From 20 through 6 meters we should use the T50-6 (yellow) toroid cores for best circuit Q (quality factor).

It is not uncommon to encounter parasitic or self-oscillations in a high-gain RF amplifier. Such spurious oscillations may occur at audio, LF, MF, HF, VHF or UHF. Short connecting leads will help to reduce the chance of self-oscillation. R1 is used as a VHF/UHF parasitic suppressor. Oscillations at lower frequencies may be eliminated by "swamping" T2 with a resistance (R2). The value of this resistor may range from 1K to 10K. R2 will lower the Q of the tuned transformer, thereby reducing the selectivity. For this reason we should use the highest value of resistance that will stabilize the amplifier. An advantage of the use of R2 is that the response of the T2 tuned circuit will be broader than if no resistor were used. This permits peak signal response across a wider portion of a band than would otherwise be possible. It can be seen that various tradeoffs exist in the general design of an RF amplifier.

The gain of the circuit at A of Fig. 1-3 may be as great as 15 or 18 dB, whereas the circuit of Fig. 1-3B will yield only 10-12 dB of gain in an average case. A virtue of the grounded-gate FET RF amplifier is stability, assuming the gate lead to the point of grounding is very short. VHF or UHF parasitics can still occur, so we have included R1 for that reason. R2 can be added if other forms of self-oscillation take place. T1 and T2 follow the same rules set forth for the amplifier of Fig. 1-3A, except that the FET source tap is approximately 1/4 the total secondary turns. This amplifier has been a favorite of mine for many years. Additional gain ahead of the PD may be obtained by using two of these amplifiers in cascade (series). However, the extra gain is seldom advantageous. In fact, too much gain ahead of a mixer or PD can impair the dynamic range seriously.

1.5 Audio Channel

We may tend to think that the audio section of a DC receiver is of no special significance, provided it assures ample overall gain for the receiver (75 to 100 dB). This is not a wise philosophy if we are seeking high performance. Why? Because the good qualities of a well-designed front end can be spoiled by an inferior audio strip. What features should we consider? First, a low distortion amplifier is necessary if we don't want fuzzy-sounding signals in the headphones or speaker. Crossover distortion is often the cause of poor audio, and the weaker the signal being received the more annoying the "fuzz" caused by the distortion. Some audio ICs are prone to having crossover distortion, and there is no means available to alter the internal biasing to correct the problem. I prefer to use discrete devices because I have control over the bias applied to the output transistors. I have found, however, that many low-power audio ICs, such as the LM-386, are relatively clean in terms of distortion.

Some attention needs to be paid to audio shaping (frequency response) when designing a receiver. That is, we want to pass only those frequencies that are useful in communicating. For SSB reception (to reduce the effects of QRM) the frequency response of the receiver should be from 300 to 2500 or 3000 Hz for best results. When designing for CW reception the overall response should be narrow, and it should peak at our preferred beat-note frequency. The commercial standard these days calls for a peak CW-note response of roughly 700-800 Hz. All frequencies above and below that range should be rolled off sharply.

Noise figure is important also in our receiver audio strip. The lower the front-end gain of the DC receiver the more important this consideration becomes. As a matter of design practice I always use a low-noise transistor audio amplifier immediately after the PD or the filter that follows the PD. The benefits of a low NF in the audio channel are especially prominent when copying weak signals. A high NF will mask a weak signal in hiss noise. An MPF102 or equivalent JFET serves nicely as a low-noise audio preamplifier.

1.6 DC Receiver Selectivity

The dedicated QRP operator could not survive for long without overall receiver selectivity: The QRM would render reception almost impossible during periods of high activity. How might we obtain the needed CW or SSB selectivity for a DC receiver? Well, two methods are in use today -- the addition of a passive LC filter, or the use of an RC active filter. These filters are designed for use in the audio section of the DC receiver. Generally, the audio filter is inserted directly after the low-noise audio preamp which follows the PD. However, some amateurs add the filter between the headphone jack and the phones, external to the receiver. The shortcoming of that technique is that high audio levels can over-load an active filter, causing distortion and poor performance in general. Ideally, the filter should be used at some low-level point in the audio system.

Fig. 1-4 shows a passive CW filter at illustration A. An RC (res-istor/capacitor) active filter is shown at B of Fig. 1-4.

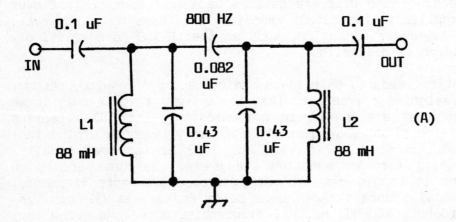

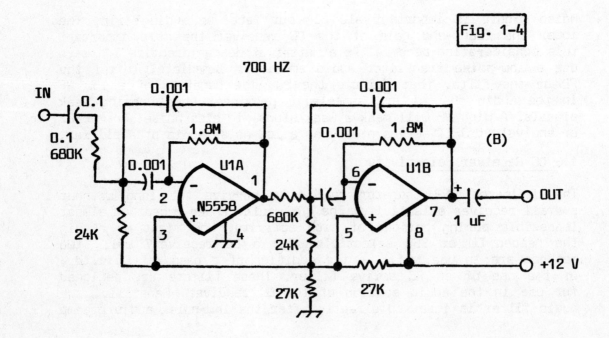

Fig. 1-4

The passive filter uses two 88-mH telephone toroids (surplus). If these can't be found you may order two of the large Amidon Assoc. pot-core blanks (2000 or 2500 permeability) and easily wind your own 88-mH inductors. Winding instructions are supplied with the pot cores. The capacitors used in Fig. 1-4A should be high-Q types, such as polystyrene or mylar. The values specified may be difficult to locate. If so, you may parallel various values of capacitor to obtain the specified capacitance. Alternatively, the 0.43-uF units can be replaced with 0.47-uF capacitors, and the 0.082 capacitor can be changed to 0.1 uF. There will be minor variations in performance if these changes are made. Two of these filters may be used in series to sharpen the skirts of the response curve, but with added insertion loss as a penalty.

The RC active filter of Fig. 1-4B uses an 8-pin DIP dual op amp to provide a two-pole, 700-Hz format. Three poles (one more identical filter section) will provide sharper skirts. But, for most CW operation the two-pole circuit is adequate. All of the capacitors other than the input and output blocking units are high-Q types. Polystyrene capacitors are recommended. They should be closely matched in value to ensure a narrow nose response for the filter. It is important also to use closely matched resistors in the circuit. Normally, 5% units will suffice.

Most of the older op-amp ICs generate internal noise that is referred to as "popcorn hash." It is better, therefore, to use one of the newer op amps that contain FETs at the input, such as the Radio Shack TLO series of op amps. These are very quiet chips.

Both of the filters shown in Fig. 1-4 are practical designs. They represent the starting point in filter complexity. Sharper filters may appeal to you. If so, the **ARRL Handbook** and **Solid State Design** contain specific design data, plus examples of more elaborate filters, passive and active. The filters shown here are more than adequate for most simple QRP gear.

1.7 LO Considerations

Stability of the tunable oscillator is as important to a DC receiver as it is to a high-performance superhet. The greater the overall selectivity of the receiver the more important becomes frequency stability. A wandering LO will cause the received signal to disappear from the receiver passband.

Also, the LO output should not contain high amounts of harmonic energy. The harmonic responses should be 40 dB or greater below the peak output of the desired LO energy. I like to use a simple half-wave harmonic filter at the LO output port to help ensure spectral purity. If harmonics are present, the receiver will respond to signals outside the band of interest, thereby causing all manner of unnecessary QRM.

Fig. 1-5 shows two approaches we may consider when designing our VBFO. The circuit of Fig. 1-5A indicates how simple it is to build a variable crystal oscillator (VXO). Excellent long-term stability is characteristic of VXOs, even during significant changes in ambient temperature. The negative qualities of the VXO are limited tuning range, which worsens as the operating frequency is lowered. For example, a typical frequency swing at 3.5 MHz might be 3 kHz, whereas at 14 MHz it is easy to obtain shifts of 10 kHz or greater. The other problem with VXOs is nonlinear tuning by means of C3. As C3 becomes fully meshed (max. capacitance end), the change in frequency slows down, but near the minimum capacitance end of the C3 tuning range, the frequency changes rapidly. This problem is more annoying when the VXO is used in a receiver, than when it is used to control the transmitter frequency.

AT-cut fundamental crystals in HC-6/U holders seem to have the greatest frequency swing in a VXO. The lower the stray capacitance in the oscillator circuit, the greater the swing possible. Therefore, the capacitance of C1 and C2 should be as low as possible, consistent with ample feedback to start the oscillator. NPO or dipped silver-mica capacitors are best at C1 and C2. L1 is required for large frequency changes. I suggest 10 uH for 15 to 20 MHz crystals, 20 uH for 7 to 15 MHz operation, and 40 uH for 3.5 MHz VXOs. Slug-tuned or toroidal coils are suitable at L1, provided the unloaded Q is 50 or greater. The VXO crystal should be etched for the upper end of the desired operating range. As C3 is adjusted for greater capacitance, the VXO operating frequency will move lower.

A simple LC VBFO is illustrated in Fig. 1-5B. A Colpitts circuit of this type offers good frequency stability if certain precautions are taken. The principal "sensitive" components are C1-C6, plus L1. NPO ceramic (disc or dogbone) capacitors are recommended for C1-C4, but good results have been obtained with polystyrene capacitors. Silver-mica capacitors have been used successfully by many amateurs, but one can't predict whether a given silver-mica unit will exhibit zero, negative or positive drift with changes in internal temperature. I have been successful in obtaining stable VFO operation by the "cut-and-try" method. Specifically, it requires trying various silver-mica capacitors, one at a time, then running a VFO drift test after each change. It can be tedious experimenting!

In an ideal VFO we would use an air-wound coil with stiff tubing or wire for L1. The coil turns would be unable to move. Unfortunately, a coil of that kind would be impractical in a solid-state rig. Modern tunable oscillators contain coils that have some form of magnetic core, fixed or adjustable. As the ambient temperature changes, there will be shifts in the core permeability. This increases or decreases the coil inductance, which leads to drift. No. 6 powdered iron (code yellow) seems to be rather stable. It is suggested for slug-tuned or toroidal VFO inductors. A coating of Q Dope is recommended to

12

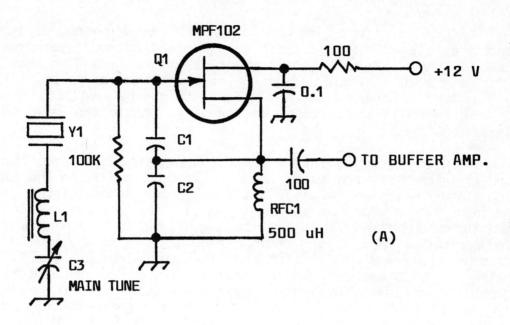

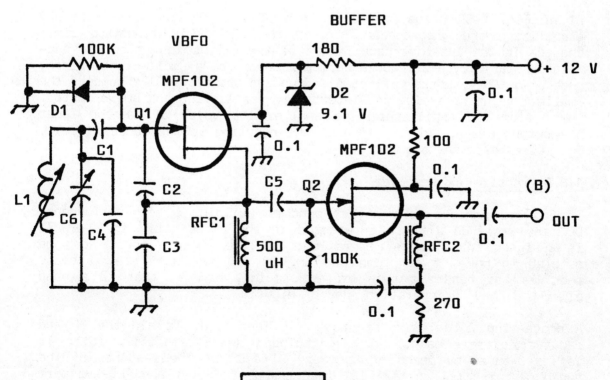

FIG. 1-5

affix the coil turns to the core. It is best to use the largest wire gauge practical when winding a VFO inductor. This will aid the coil Q and will improve the mechanical stability of the coil.

All tunable oscillators should be followed by a buffer or buffer-amplifier stage. This will help to isolate the oscillator from the load, thereby eliminating unwanted "pulling" of the frequency when load conditions change. I have found a JFET source-follower to be a good buffer. Output from Q2 of Fig. 1-5B can be amplified by means of a bipolar-transistor stage or stages to obtain the required LO-injection level.

Regulated dc operating voltage should be applied to the oscillator, and it makes good sense to regulate the voltage applied to the following stage (buffer) to minimize load changes at the oscillator output. Further improvements in stability can be realized by placing the tunable oscillator and its related amplifiers in a separate shield compartment or box. This technique aids in keeping stray RF energy from entering the VFO and causing frequency instability. It also helps to keep the ambient temperature around the oscillator more constant. An acceptable Amateur Radio VFO should not drift more than 100 Hz after a 10-minute warmup. Normally, the greatest drift, known as "short-term drift," takes place the first 5 or 10 minutes after operating voltage is applied. This is caused by internal heating of the VFO components, brought on by RF current flowing through them.

D1 of Fig. 1-5B clips positive peaks of the RF sine wave, thereby stabilizing the transconductance of the FET. This tends to limit changes in the internal capacitance of the FET, which helps the osc-illator stability and reduces harmonic currents. A small-signal diode, such as a 1N914, works well at D1. Coupling capacitor C1 should be the smallest value possible, consistent with oscillation and ample output power from the oscillator. The smaller the value of C1 the lower the output power, but the lighter the coupling to the tuned circuit. This also helps the stability.

1.8 A Practical DC Receiver

If you are anxious to try your hand at building a high-performance DC receiver, you will be interested in the circuit of Fig. 1-6. It is designed for 40-meter operation, but the tuned circuits can be altered to make it function on 160, 80, 30 or 20 meters. I chose the 40-meter band for this project, mainly because that is a good all-round band for operation, day or night.

A diode-ring PD is used for high DR. Therefore, to aid the NF and receiver overall gain, we have included an RF amplifier (Q1). It is fixed-tuned by means of trimmers C1 and C2. The response of the tuned circuits (T1 and T2) is broad enough to cover any 100-kHz part of the 40-meter band without a significant gain loss.

13

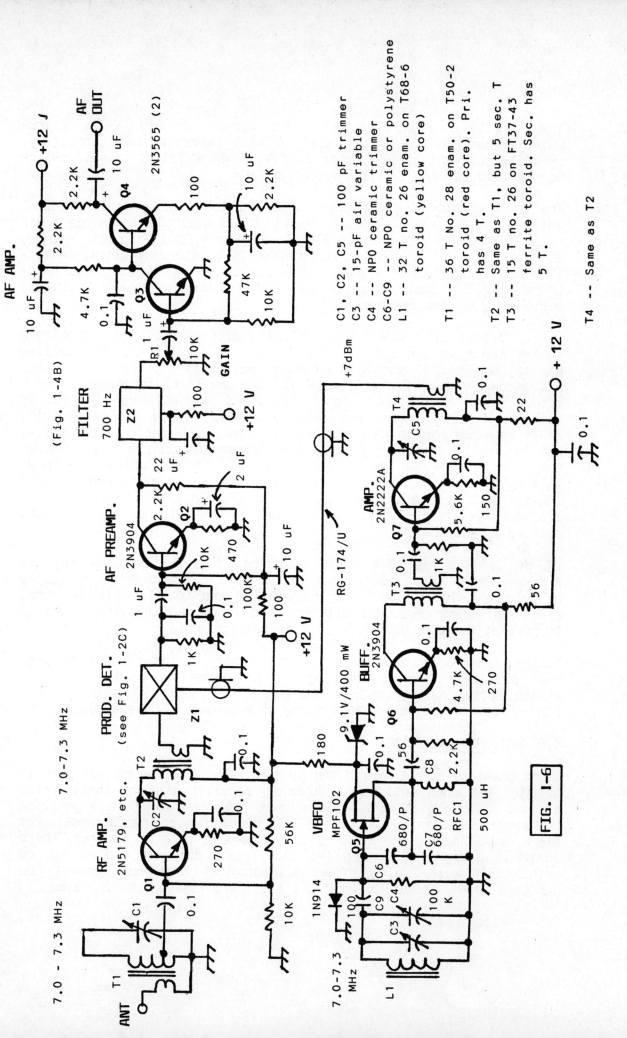

FIG. 1-6

The PD (Z1) is a duplication of the circuit in Fig. 1-2C. A low-noise AF preamp (Q2) follows the PD. Next comes the CW filter (Z2), which is the same circuit found in Fig. 1-4B. A filter of your choice may be used for Z1.

The audio filter is followed by a simple fed-back AF amplifier that was popularized some years ago by W7ZOI. It will provide ample audio power for hi-Z headphones on signals that are S3 or better. You may wish to add a 741 op-amp amplifier after Q4 to aid weak-signal reception. An LM386 would be a good choice for use after Q4, if added head-phone level is desired, or if you wish to drive a speaker with the audio strip of the receiver.

The VBFO (Q5) uses a JFET in a Colpitts arrangement. The approximate tuning range of the VBFO is 7.0 to 7.3 MHz. There is some overlap at each end of that range. The output from Q5 is amplified by a Class A broadband stage, Q6. A 2N2222A is used at Q7 to increase the VBFO output power to +7 dBm, which is required by the diode-ring PD. No harmonic filter is used for this oscillator strip: The selectivity of T4 is ample for "laundering" the LO signal. Greater waveform purity may be had by inserting a half-wave filter (50 ohm, Q = 1) between the secondary of T4 and the input of Z1. If the distance between T4 and Z1 is a few inches or greater, use miniature shielded cable (RG-174/U) to route the LO voltage from T4. This will be the proper procedure if the VBFO strip is enclosed in a shield box, as suggested earlier in the text.

If the receiver is to be used also for SSB reception, you may add a two-pole, double-throw switch at Z2 for the purpose of inserting or removing the audio filter between Q2 and Q3. If this is done, a 1-uF blocking capacitor will be needed between the switch and Q2 to prevent shorting out the collector voltage of Q2.

Transistor substitutions may be made throughout the circuit of Fig. 1-6, provided the specifications of the substitute units equal or exceed those of the devices indicated. For example, a 2N4416 FET can be used for Q5, and a 2N2222 may be employed at Q2 and Q6.

1.9 THE SUPERHETERODYNE

It is possible to not exceed the simplicity of the DC-receiver circuit of Fig. 1-6 when building a superhet receiver that has only a few stages. We can eliminate many of the features found in high-price commercial receivers, while still achieving good performance. For example, AGC is not needed, nor do we need to have an S meter. There is no pressing need for an I-F or RF gain control, and we can do rather well with analog rather than digital frequency readout We can pass up the conveniences of I-F shift and passband tuning also

Our objective in QRP receiving is to have a superhet that is frequency stable, sensitive, adequate in terms of overall gain and selective enough to reject most of the QRM near the desired frequency of interest. These objectives are attainable with modest circuitry, just as they are when designing a DC recv v r. The major advantages of the superhet are <u>single-signal</u> reception a response on only one side of zero beat) and relative immunity to the common ills of the DC receiver (hum and microphonics). Despite the differences in the design and performance of the two receiver types, a superhet follows the same general design rules. Fig. 1-7 shows the format of a superheterodyne receiver by way of a block diagram.

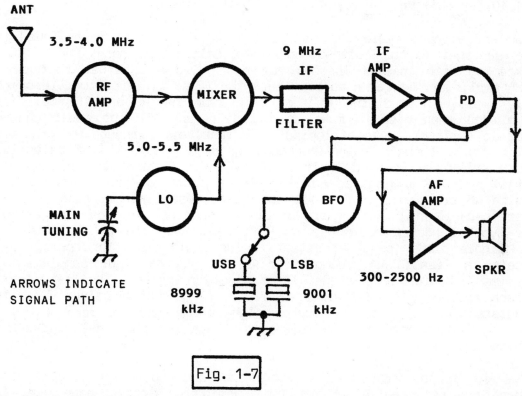

Fig. 1-7

The bare essentials of a superhet are indicated above. Many frequency combinations are possible for the IF and LO portions of a superhet receiver. Those indicated are for discussion purposes only. Such frills as AGC, frequency synthesis, band switching and an S meter are excluded from the block diagram in order to simplify the drawing.

Typically, the IF filter would have a bandwidth (BW) of approximately 2.4 kHz for SSB reception. The CW bandwidth is usually 500 or 250 Hz. Separate filters are required for each bandwidth. This requires a switching arrangement for the filters.

The mixer and/or PD of a superhet may be passive or active, depending upon the design objectives and the overall gain capability of the receiver. As is the case with a DC receiver, a superhet needs about 100 dB of overall gain to ensure ample audio-output power for weak-signal reception. The superhet differs significantly from the DC receiver in terms of where the gain is acquired: The DC receiver depends on a high-gain audio channel, whereas the superhet develops most of its gain in the IF section -- typically 40 to 60 dB of IF amplification. In planning a design we must take into account the losses of RF filters, IF filters and passive mixers. These losses must be deducted from the combined gain of the active RF, IF and AF stages in order to determine the receiver overall gain.

1.10 Superhet Complexity

We are already aware that AGC and other extras may be excluded from a superhet circuit without severe penalties to good operation. In keeping with this philosophy, we can build a superhet that has no RF amplifier. We may also eliminate the IF amplifiers (two are common-ly employed). With the loss of gain from the RF and IF amplifiers, we will then need to make up the difference in the audio channel, as is customary when designing a DC receiver. Although we may choose the "bare bones" design concept, good sensitivity and selectivity can still be achieved. This will call for a low-noise mixer, an IF filter and a low-noise audio-amplifier section. Most of the pocket-size AM transistor radios fit the "bare bones" description, but they are capable of providing acceptable to good performance. For example, a typical pocket radio has no RF stage, only one IF amplifier, and a single diode (passive) detector. The audio amplifier normally con-tains a transistor preamplifier and a push-pull or complementary-symmetry audio-output stage. If we consider the small built-in ferrite loop antenna, the performance of the AM pocket receiver is rather outstanding, even on the weaker signals. There is no reason why we cannot adopt similar techniques of frugality when building a ham-band superhet.

We may, in the interest of saving money and shortening assembly time, modify a pocket-size AM broadcast radio for amateur-band use. This involves removing the loop antenna and replacing it with a toroidal inductor (to reduce pickup of 0.5 to 1.6-MHz signals), adding a BFO, and providing for IF selectivity. An outboard ham-band converter is then used ahead of the pocket radio. Detailed information about this scheme of doing things may be found in "A Semi-Kit Receiver for 75/80 Meters," by W1FB, **QST** for August, 1985.

The real nitty-gritty of superhet-receiver design, simple and com-plex, is given in simple language in ARRL's **Solid State Design** by W7ZOI and W1FB. No QRPer should be without that book.

Let's look now at a suggested circuit for a simple superhet receiver.

1.11 A No-Frills Superhet

Although the circuit of Fig. 1-8 is designed for 40-meter use, it can be modified easily (by experienced builders) for use on 160, 80 or 30 meters. Only L1, L2 and the LO feedback capacitors need to be changed. Operation above 30 meters is not recommended because an RF amplifier would be required, and the 455-kHz IF (low) would cause unwanted image responses with so simple an input tuned circuit (L1-C1).

This circuit represents what I consider the bare necessities for a simple superhet. A single series crystal provides IF selectivity (Y1) that is surprisingly adequate for most CW work. Only one stage of IF amplification (Q2) is used, and there is no AGC. Audio preamplifier Q4 needs to be followed by additional amplifier stages. You may use the fed-back audio amplifier (Q3 and Q4) of Fig. 1-6 to obtain more than sufficient headphone volume. An LM386 audio IC could also be used after Q4 of Fig. 1-8. A 10K-ohm audio-gain control should be used between Q4 and the successive audio stages.

C1 is used as a preselector peaking control (panel mounted). C4 is the main tuning control. A vernier drive is needed to ensure smooth and easy frequency adjustment. There will be slight oscillator pulling when C1 is adjusted, but it presents no problems once the front end is peaked for maximum signal response.

The BFO (Q6) is an LC type to minimize cost. A 455-kHz IF transformer serves as the tuned circuit, with the secondary winding connected to provide feedback. The slug in T3 is tuned for the desired CW beat note, then affixed with a drop of wax to prevent movement from vibration. D3 is used to obtain 9.1 V, regulated.

You may use other dual-gate MOSFETs in place of Q1 and Q3, such as 3N211 or 3N212. A dual-gate MOSFET may be used at Q5 by tying the gates in parallel and using the circuit shown. The secondary windings of T1 and T2 are not used in this circuit.

A 9-MHz IF may be used with this general scheme. If so, 10.7-MHz IF transformers may be substituted for T1, T2 and T3. The addition of a small value of external capacitance will bring the transformers down to 9 MHz. This circuit serves as a nice basis for experimenting. Countless refinements and changes are possible. For example, you can tailor the circuit for 80-meter operation, then use down-converters to provide reception on the higher bands. This would make it a simple matter to realize 20, 15, 12 and 10-meter operation.

L2 should be coated with two layers of polystyrene Q Dope or some equivalent high-dielectric cement. This will enhance the mechanical stability of the tuned circuit.

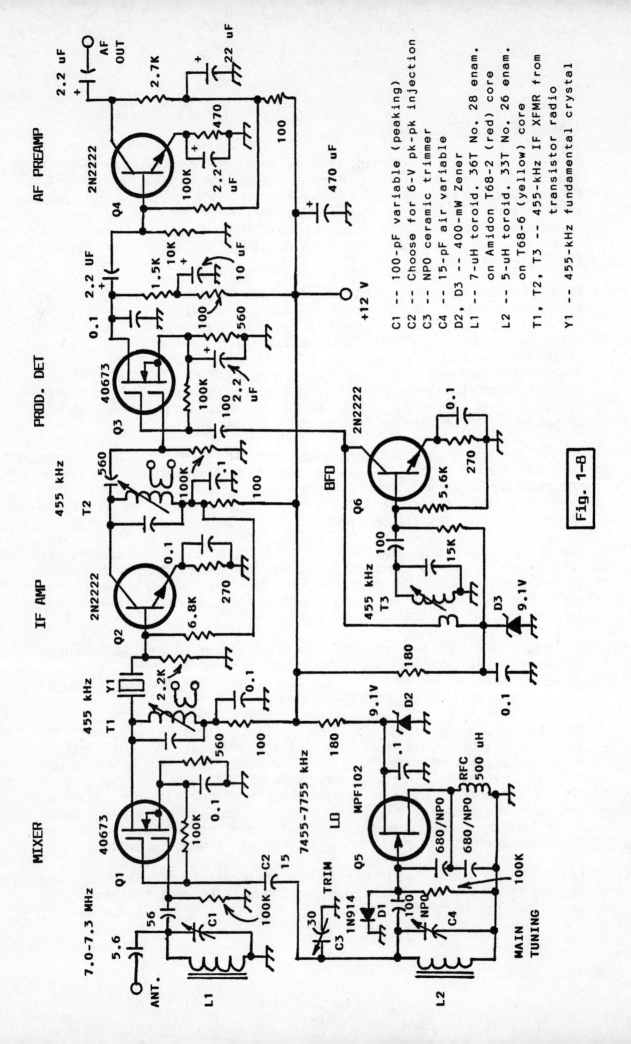

Fig. 1-8

1.12 **A Medium-Grade Superhet**

Excellent selectivity and a highly stable LO are the main features of the 20-meter superhet of Fig. 1-9. The VXO permits coverage of roughly 30 kHz of the 20-meter band. Switchable crystals can be used to cover all of the CW band.

This circuit is an improved version of the "Bare Bones Superhet," W1FB, **QST** for June, 1982. It also uses some of the better features found in the "Mini-Miser's Dream Receiver," W1FB, **QST** for Sept. 1976. PC boards and parts kits for those two **QST** receivers are available from Circuit Board Specialists, Box 969, Pueblo, CO 81002.

The heart of the receiver in Fig. 1-9 is FL1, which is a 260-Hz CW filter made from low-cost Radio Shack 3.579-MHz color-burst crystals. The filter is a ladder type for which the constants were developed by W7ZOI. Because of the sharp response of the filter, a very stable LO is required -- hence the VXO (Q3).

You may select your own audio-amplifier channel for headphone or speaker operation. The fed-back, two-transistor audio section for the DC receiver in this chapter can be added after Q6 if you plan to use phones. Alternatively, an LM386 IC may be added after Q6 for headphone or speaker use.

Y1 is a fundamental crystal, 30-pF load capacitance, in an HC-6/U holder. Y2 is a Radio Shack color-burst crystal, as in FL1. C5 rubbers Y2 to the upper side of the FL1 passband for a peak response of 700 Hz for CW reception. The overall receiver gain, as shown, is approximately 65 dB. A 0.1-uV signal at the input to Q1 produces a plainly audible response at the receiver output. Fig. 1-10 shows the circuit for FL1 of Fig. 1-9.

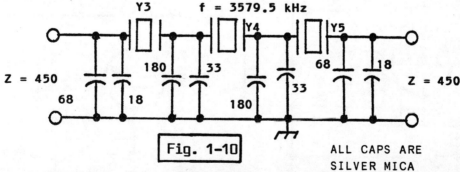

Fig. 1-10

ALL CAPS ARE
SILVER MICA

The final value for C7 should be chosen to provide 4 to 6 V pk-pk at gate 2 of Q2. This will ensure a good compromise between mixer conversion gain and minimum IMD. Do <u>not</u> exceed <u>6 V pk-pk, as greater voltage can damage Q2.</u> T2 and T3 are transformer foundations that are available from Amidon Assoc.

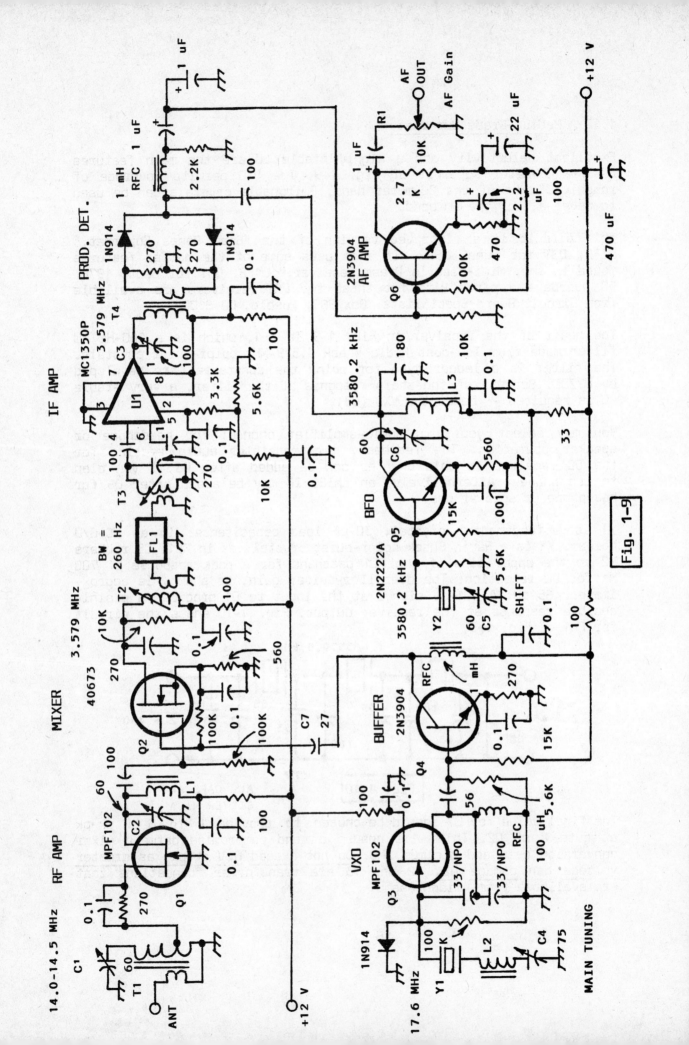

Fig. 1-9

There is no reason why the circuit of Fig. 1-9 can't be modified for use on bands other than 80 meters. 75- or 80-meter use is not practical because of the IF falling in the 80-meter band. But, the input tuned circuits can be changed for other frequencies, and a VFO can be substituted for the VXO circuit provided. For example, you could build the receiver for 40-meter use, then provide coverage of 30, 20, 15, 12 and 10 meters by means of outboard down-converters. The key components are described below in Table 1.

TABLE 1

Part No.

C1, C2, C5, C6 -- Miniature plastic or ceramic trimmer
C3 -- Mica trimmer.
C4 -- Miniature air variable, 75 pF, panel mounted.
C7 -- See text. Selected value.
L2 -- Toroidal 6-uH inductor. 36T no. 26 enam. on
      Amidon T50-6 (yellow) core.
L1 -- Toroidal inductor, 2.6 uH. Use 25T of no. 28
      enam. wire on T50-6 core.
L3 -- Toroidal inductor, 9 uH. Use 13T of no. 24 enam.
      wire on an Amidon FT37-61 ferrite core.
R1 -- Audio-taper carbon control, panel mount.
RFC -- All are miniature, iron-core types.
T1 -- Toroidal transformer, 2.6 uH. Use 25T of no. 28
      enam. wire on T50-6 core. Tap 6T above ground.
      Primary consists or 2T of no. 28 wire.
T2, T3 -- 4.7:1 turns ratio, 6.5 uH. Use 27T of no. 28
      enam. wire on bobbin of Amidon (Micrometals) L57-2
      xfrm. assembly. Links have 6T.
T4 -- Toroidal transformer, 26 uH. Use 20T of no. 26
      enam. wire on FT50-61 (125 perm.). Sec. has 5T.
U1 -- Motorola RF/IF IC.
Y1, Y2 -- See text.

The Amidon powdered-iron toroids are manufactured by Micrometals Corp., and the ferrite toroids are made by Fair-Rite Corp. You may cross-reference other brands of toroid cores by sending for data on the two commercial cores mentioned here. Data on both brands of toroid core are available in the W1FB Prentice-Hall book, **Ferromagnetic Core Design & Application Handbook**, no. 0-13-314088-1, Englewood Cliffs, NJ 07632 (also available from a CA vendor, Amidon Assoc., 12033 Otsego St., N. Hollywood, CA 91607. Phone (213) 760-4429. The book is written in plain language and deals with toroids, pot cores, rods and sleeves. Many practical circuits are included.

1.13 HF Converters

Earlier in the chapter we considered the use of converters to provide additional band access with our QRP receivers. Proper design for high-performance follows the same rules set forth for high-performance receivers. That is, if high dynamic range is desired, attention must be paid to mixer design and gain distribution in the converter. However, for most of our QRP operations we can obtain good performance with fairly simple converter designs. The main consideration is to limit the overall converter gain to slightly more than unity. A converter gain of 5 to 10 dB is adequate. Too much converter gain will cause degradation of the main receiver (tunable IF) dynamic range because of high signal levels being applied to the RF amplifier and or mixer of the main receiver.

Elaborate converters can be designed and used, but those are somewhat beyond the scope of this book. We will consider a simple design that you can use as a basis for various frequency schemes. Our practical model is designed for a tunable IF of 7.0 to 7.3 MHz, since most QRPers have little receivers for the 40-meter band. The circuit of Fig. 1-11 can be used ahead of a DC or superhet receiver.

1.14 Practical HF-Band Converter

A grounded-gate FET is used as the RF amplifier in Fig. 1-11. It provides between 10 and 12 dB of gain, and it has a low NF. The dual-gate MOSFET mixer (Q2) has a conversion gain of 6 to 10 dB as configured. A broadband output circuit is used for the purpose of simplifying the interface between the mixer and the input of the main receiver (T2). Q3 operates as a 3rd-overtone oscillator. C2 should not be necessary unless the crystal (Y1) is sluggish, in which case only 5 to 10 pF should be required.

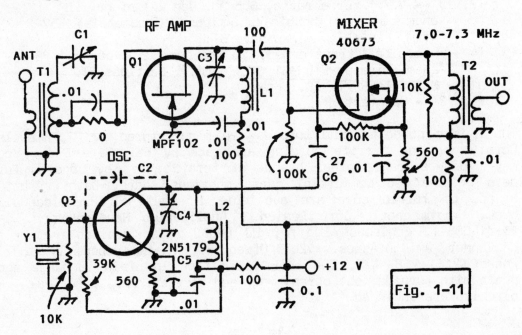

C1, C3 abd C4 of Fig. 1-11 are 60-pF miniature trimmers. They may be mica, ceramic or plastic units. A ball-park value is given (27 pF) for C6. The correct value is such that gate 2 of Q2 has 4-6 V pk-pk of LO injection. You may need to experiment with the value of C6 to obtain the proper injection voltage.

Q1 can be any JFET with VHF ratings, such as the 2N4416 family of transistors. A 3N211 or 3N212 can be used at Q2. Any UHF npn transistor is suitable for Q3. The fT should be at least 1000 MHz.

Y1 can be "netted" to provide accurate readout of the converter frequency on the station receiver. If this feature is desired, install a 60-pF trimmer in series with the crystal at the grounded end of Y1. If this does not move the crystal frequency in the desired direction, try using the trimmer in parallel with the crystal. If parallel operation causes the oscillator to cease operating, you may need to add C2 and/or experiment with the value of the feedback capacitor, C5. The input and output impedance (Z) of this converter is 50 ohms. This makes it easy to switch two or more converters (input, output and +12-V lines) ahead of the main receiver for multiband coverage.

TABLE 2

BAND	C5 pF	L1	L2	T1	T2
30M	47	6uH, 35T no. 28 on T50-2 toroid.	2uH, 22T no. 28 on T50-6 toroid.	6uH, 35T no. 28 on T50-2 toroid. Tap 8T from gnd. Pri - 3T.	15T no. 26 on a ferrite FT50-43 toroid. 3T sec.
20M	39	3.2uH, 28T no. 28 on T50-6 core.	1.4uH, 19T no. 26 on T50-6 core.	3.2uH, 28T no. 28 on T50-6 core. Tap 7T from gnd. Pri,3T	same
15M	27	1.4uH, 18T no. 26 on T50-6 core.	0.8uH, 14T no. 24 on T50-6 core.	Same as L1, tap 4T, Pri, 2T.	same

Y1 -- 17.15 MHz (30M); 21.3 MHz (20M); 28.23 MHz (15M)

CHAPTER 2

THE WORLD OF QRP TRANSMITTERS

Quality performance is as important to QRP transmitting as it
is to receiving. Some QRP operators insist upon such circuit simplicity that transmitter performance is shabby. Some feel that
the term "QRP" denotes crude, inexpensive circuits that can be
built solely from junk parts. This is a poor philosophy for any
amateur who takes pride in his or her equipment and operating
procedures. This does not imply that a low-cost QRP transmitter
is incapable of delivering a clean signal. Many one-tube or one-
transistor oscillators have produced acceptable on-the-air signals, but some poorly designed ones have created TVI, chirpy signals, hum on the carrier and spurious output frequencies that
fell in the HF spectrum.

Pride in the signal quality should be a rule for any ham-radio
operator, irrespective of the power level. Furthermore, the cleaner
the QRP signal the more effective we will be in luring other operators into a QSO: Some hams will not enter into a QSO with a guy
or gal that has a cruddy signal. A stigma, deserved or not, is
attached to an operator with a bum signal. Such people are referred to as "lids."

It should be a matter of practice to never put a new QRP rig on
the air until we have listened to the signal on a receiver while
operating the rig into a dummy load. There should be a pure note
that is free of hum or chirp. Also, we do not want our CW note
to be clicky on the make or break of the key. Key clicks can cause
severe interference above and below the operating frequency, even
when we are using QRP power levels. I have found that a CW note
which is a bit "hard" on the leading edge of the waveform (but
not clicky) will give a QRP signal the "presence" it needs to
break through the noise and QRM, when a soft CW note will fail
to get through. So, don't make a valiant effort to have a classic
CW waveform. Too soft a note (like a bell ringing) will not only
be hard to copy, but it can be impossible to copy at the higher
CW speeds.

This chapter is dedicated to design objectives, along with data
concerning solutions to common problems in QRP transmitters. We
will emphasize spectral purity by showing simple harmonic filters
that can be used at the transmitter output.

2.1 Starting with the Oscillator

The crystal oscillator or VFO represent the core of any QRP rig. It is in this area of the circuit that the roots of bad signals exist. Hum, frequency drift and chirp are generally caused by improper oscillator operation. Therefore, let's concentrate on oscillators and how they function. We will also look at ways to make them function reliably in QRP circuits.

The basic name of the game in oscillator design is "feedback." Too little feedback causes erratic performance and chirp. Too much feedback causes crystal overheating (excessive current) and drift. It can also cause spurious oscillations, and in the case of an overtone oscillator we may find our crystals operating on the fundamental, rather than the desired overtone frequency.

Another common cause of oscillator instability (notably chirp) is poor isolation from the succeeding stage or stages of a transmitter. As the load conditions shift (as when the next stage is keyed), oscillator "pulling" occurs, thereby shifting the operating frequency. Light coupling to the load, plus proper feedback ratios go a long way to minimize this problem. A quality crystal is also necessary to ensure stability. Surplus crystals -- especially WW-II FT-243 types -- are often sluggish, which causes all manner of problems. I find that modern plated crystals in metal holders work the best in my circuits. I am not sounding the death knell for FT-243 crystals, for some of them work well, especially after they have been taken apart and cleaned with hot soap and water, then rinsed with clean hot water. The spring-brass contacts for the metal plates (and the plates) within the crystal holder should also be cleaned if the crystal is sluggish.

I find also that the proper choice of transistor in the VFO or crystal oscillator is important. The objectives are high ac beta (gain) and a high upper-frequency rating (fT). Most transistors can be made to oscillate at their fT or slightly higher, but they will not be reliable or efficient. Therefore, I suggest an fT of five or ten times the proposed operating frequency. For example, for a 14-MHz oscillator I make sure the transistor fT is 140 MHz or higher.

2.2 Oscillator Power

In an effort to simplify the circuit of a QRP transmitter, some ham operators attempt to extract high power from the oscillator. They feel this will reduce the number of stages needed to acquire the desired output power. Although this philosophy may be correct, excessive oscillator power causes heating that leads to drift and potential damage to the crystal. It is better to use the least oscillator power practicable, then build up the output power by means of low-cost amplifier stages. Low oscillator dc input power ensures the best frequency stability in most cases.

2.3 Common Crystal Oscillators

Perhaps there has been no circuit that was named after more people than was the crystal or LC oscillator. Such persons as Colpitts, Pierce, Franklin, Clapp, Barkhausen, Kurtz and a host of others rose to overnight fame by developing specific oscillator circuits. We will concentrate on only those oscillators that are in widespread use for amateur circuits. Some of these oscillators, along with their circuit variations are depicted in Fig. 2-1.

Fig. 2-1A shows a Pierce oscillator built around a bipolar transistor, such as a 2N2222A or 2N5179. RFC1 is an RF choke that is self-resonant (with stray circuit capacitance) below the chosen operating frequency. We may assume roughly 10 pF of stray capacitance in most circuits. Thus, for operation at 3.5 MHz we will choose an RF choke that has 1 mH or greater inductance (XL should equal 22,000 ohms or more). C1 and C2 are feedback capacitors. The XC of C2 is 455 ohms, which yields 100 pF at 3.5 MHz. C1 has a capacitive reactance (XC) of 1500 ohms, approximately. This equates to roughly 30 pF at 3.5 MHz. A trimmer is indicated for C1 to permit adjusting the feedback for best operating characteristics, consistent with the gain of the transistor and the activity of Y1. Later, we may replace the trimmer with a fixed-value capacitor of the optimum value. C3 should be of low capacitance to minimize loading of the oscillator by the circuits that follow it. Values of 10 to 50 pF are typical at 3.5 MHz (XC = 1000 ohms) C1 is adjusted for reliable oscillator starting and minimum chirp when the stage is keyed.

Fig. 2-B show a Colpitts crystal oscillator that operates on the fundamental mode of Y1. C1 and C2 are feedback capacitors. The values for C1 and C2 should be kept as low as possible, consistent with proper oscillation of Y1. These capacitors are frequently of identical value, but C1 can be made smaller than C2 in most circuits. An XC of roughly 455 ohms represents a reasonable starting point, which equates to 100 pF at 3.5 MHz. C1 can be selected in value for just enough feedback to ensure fast starting of the oscillator. The output power of this oscillator is quite low. C3 should be low in value to minimize oscillator pulling (same as C3 of Fig. 2-A).

Fig. 2-C shows a JFET version of the circuit at Fig. 2A. A dual-gate MOSFET may be substituted if gates 1 and 2 are tied together to form a single-gate MOSFET. FETs may be used in all of the circuits shown in Fig. 2-1.

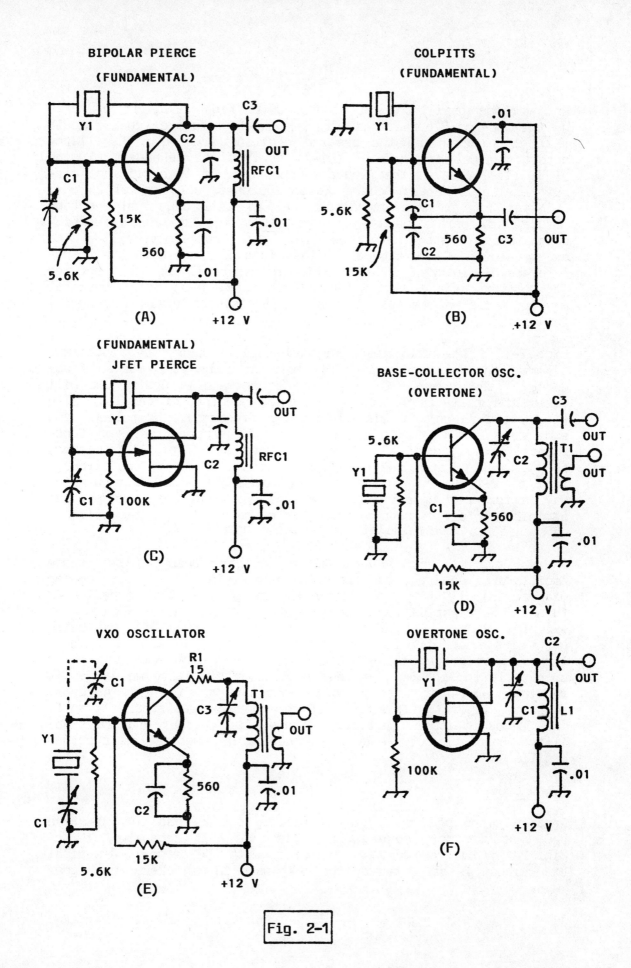

Fig. 2-1

An overtone oscillator is presented in Fig. 2-1D. It operates on the 3rd- or 5th-overtone of Y1. C2 and T1 form a tuned circuit that is resonant at the desired overtone frequency. Oscillator output may be taken via C3 (hi-Z) or from the secondary winding of T1 (lo-Z). C1 is the feedback capacitor. It is a critical circuit element. The approximate XC is 200 ohms, or 33 pF at 24 MHz. Warning: Too great a capacitance at C1 will cause an overtone crystal to operate on the fundamental mode. Additional feedback capacitance exists within the transistor (base-emitter), so the exact value of C1 must be determined in accordance with the transistor used. Fig. 2-1F shows a JFET overtone oscillator that obtains its feedback via Y1 from the output tank. A trimmer capacitor may be inserted between Y1 and the transistor drain to control the feedback voltage.

Fig. 2-1E illustrates how a crystal oscillator may be "rubbered" to move the frequency slightly above or below the marked frequency of the crystal. C1, when placed between Y1 and ground will raise the operating frequency. When connected in parallel with Y1 (dotted lines) it will lower the frequency. C2 follows the same rule as C1 of Fig. 2-1D for overtone operation. For fundamental operation of Y1, C2 should have an XC of 22 or lower, such as 1500 pF at 3.5 MHz. R1 may be used with any of the circuits in Fig. 2-1 if vhf parasitics are noted. It acts as a damping device for such unwanted oscillations. Alternatively, we may use a miniature ferrite bead (125 or 850 permeability) at the collector or drain of the oscillator to prevent parasitics.

I have avoided precise scientific design procedures for these oscillators. An ideal oscillator is not designed in the foregoing manner, but I have generalized (based on practical experience) to provide practical starting points for your convenience. For example, the bias-resistor values (base and emitter) are ballpark ones that will assure oscillation. You may want to experiment in an effort to optimize oscillator performance and power output. In the interest of best oscillator stability we can apply regulated operating voltage to the circuits of Fig. 2-1. A Zener-diode regulator (9.1V) with a 220-ohm dropping resistor will suffice, although lower operating voltages may further enhance stability. Regulation is especially desirable when using overtone oscillators.

2.4 VXO Use

Greater swing of the crystal frequency can be had when using a VXO that not only contains a series variable capacitor (C1 of Fig. 2-1E) but an inductance in series with the crystal. A typical VXO circuit is presented on the next page in Fig. 2-2. The higher

the crystal frequency the greater the frequency swing. VXOs become
desirable for portable QRP operation, where VFOs tend to drift
as a result of frequent changes in ambient temperature (weather-
related). At 20 meters, for example, shifts or 10 kHz or slightly
greater are possible with the circuit of Fig. 2-2.

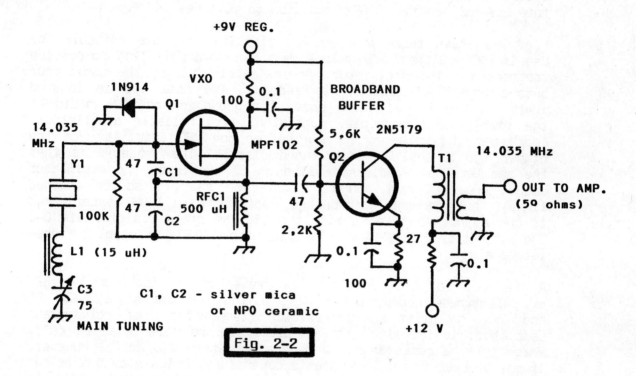

Fig. 2-2

The introduction of reactance L1 enhances the frequency shift
of Y1, which is chosen for the upper end of the desired frequency
spread. In fact, the crystal will oscillate a kHz or two above
the marked frequency when C3 is set for minimum capacitance. An
AT-cut fundamental crystal in an HC-6/U holder has provided the
greatest frequency swing in my experience. A 30-pF load capacitance is suggested for Y1 in Fig. 2-2.

Increased frequency range for Y1 can be obtained by using a greater
inductance at L1, but eventually the circuit will operate as a
VFO, and the VXO stability will be lost. A slug-tuned or toroidal
coil can be used at L1. In either case the Q of the coil should
be high (75 or greater). T1 is a broadband transformer. The primary
uses 15 turns of no. 24 enam. wire on an Amidon FT50-43 (850 ui)
ferrite toroid. The secondary winding has 5 turns.

The lower the operating frequency the less the crystal frequency
swing, with 3 kHz being about typical at 3.5 MHz.

2.5 <u>VFO Circuits and Use</u>

Many QRP applications require greater frequency coverage than can be obtained with crystal oscillators or VXOs. The simple alternative is the use of a conventional VFO. Although synthesized LOs are in step with the times, they are complex and prone to power consumption, which most QRPers would prefer to avoid. Therefore, we will confine the discussion to LC types of VFOs.

Fig. 2-3 shows three popular VFO circuits that are suitable for use in QRP equipment. Example A uses a tapped coil (L1) to provide feedback for the oscillator. Approximately 25% of the oscillator output power is required as feedback. The coil tap is located 1/4th the total coil turns above the grounded end. C3 should be the lowest value possible, consistent with reliable oscillation. The lower the value at C3 the better the VFO stability and the higher the loaded Q of the tuned circuit. The tradeoff is that the smaller the capacitance value at C3 the lower the oscillator output power. Output can be taken from the FET source (dashed lines), but reduced load-change variations will be experienced if the output is taken across the 150-ohm drain resistor via C4. The circuit of Fig. 2-3A may be used with MOSFETs or bipolar transistors also.

A standard Colpitts oscillator is presented in Fig. 2-3B. An NPO or polystyrene capacitor is best suited for use at C1, C3, C4 and C5. The drift characteristic (temperature) of polystyrene capacitors is opposite that of powdered-iron core material (L1), which in some cases tends to reduce long-term VFO drift. However, it may be best to use NPO ceramic capacitors, which stay put rather well over a wide temperature range. Obtaining minimum drift in an LC oscillator requires considerable cut-and-try effort, and can be a tedious exercise. C4 and C5 of Fig. 2-3B have an XC of roughly 45 ohms (1000 pF at 3.5 MHz), and C3 has an XC of 200 ohms (220 pF at 3.5 MHz). Again, RFC1 should be self-resonant somewhat below the VFO operating frequency.

A series-tuned Colpitts (sometimes called "Clapp") VFO is seen at C of Fig. 2-3. The advantage of the series-tuned circuit is that greater inductance is required for L1 than is needed for the circuit of Fig. 2-3B. This takes on greater importance when our VFO is used at 7 MHz and higher, where with the circuit of Fig. 2-3B we would have high C and low L. At 7 MHz and above a small inductance becomes affected by circuit wiring and PC-board foils, which constitute part of the inductor. This lowers the Q and also leads to instability from chassis flexing and vibration. C1, C2 and C3 become much smaller in value than at Fig. 2-3B, owing to the larger inductance of L1. Therefore, we may need only

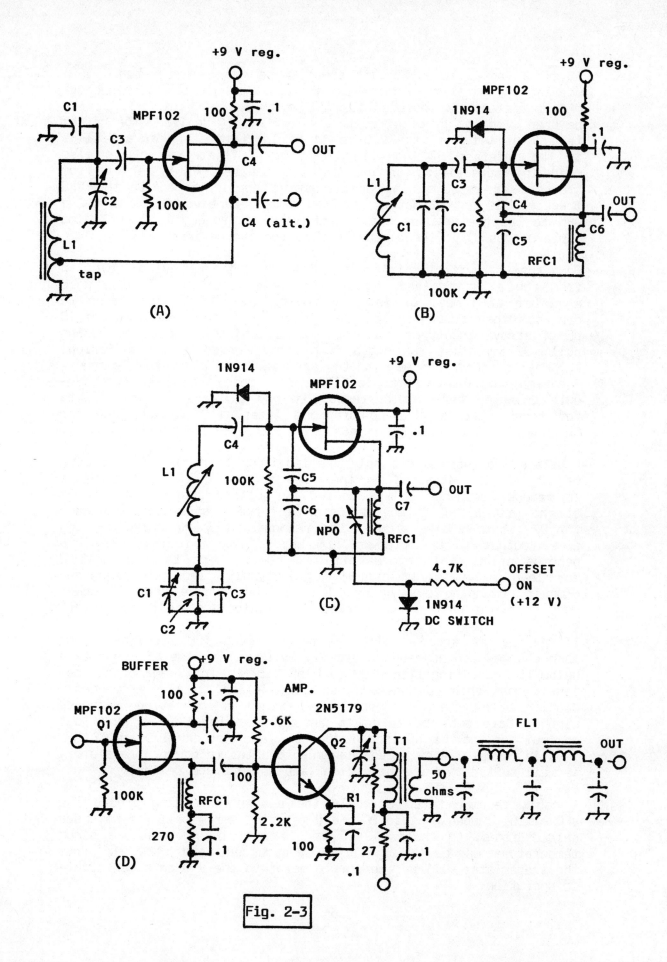

Fig. 2-3

50 pF of total tuned-circuit capacitance for a series-tuned VFO. whereas the parallel-tuned VFO might call for 150 pF. A frequency-offset circuit is included for the VFO at C of Fig. 2-3. It may be used with the other circuits in Fig. 2-3 if desired. The offset feature is vital if the VFO is to be left operating at all times in the interest of long-term stability. Offset control is also used in transceivers to provide the desired 700-Hz shift from transmit to receive. In non-transceive applications, if the VFO frequency is not offset or shifted during receive, it will cause QRM to the operator on his or her receive frequency. A switching diode places C7 in the circuit during receive periods.

Some form of buffering is needed after the VFO to provide isolation from the external load. Fig. 2-3D shows a circuit I have used a number of times. Q1 is a source-follower. RFC1 is chosen to provide broad resonance at the operating frequency, based on 10 pF of stray circuit capacitance. We may think of it as a peaking coil. Q2 amplifies the signal and provides additional buffering. FL1 may be added when we wish to "sanitize" the VFO output energy. The simple half-wave harmonic filter (low pass) will greatly atten-uate unwanted harmonic currents. It has a loaded Q of 1. Data for these filters will be provided later. FL1 is designed for 50 ohms, input and output impedance.

Regulated voltage is not only applied to Q1, but the bias network of Q2 is also attached to the +9-V regulated line. This helps to reduce frequency shifts caused by voltage changes at Q2. R1 at the primary of T1 may be used to force a collector impedance for Q2. It will also broaden the response of T1 to cause the VFO power output to be more uniform across the tuning range. This becomes of special interest below 7 MHz, where tuned-circuit Q may lead to a fairly narrow tuned-circuit frequency response. However, swamping by way of R1 will also reduce the VFO power output, since part of the power is dissipated in the resistor.

If the stages after a VFO are to be keyed (CW), chirp-causing load changes can be reduced greatly by operating the VFO an octave below the operating frequency (VFO on 3.5 MHz for 7-MHz transmiss-ions). When this is done it becomes necessary to use a frequency doubler after the VFO before amplifying the operating-frequency signal. Care must be taken to ensure that the doubler puts out maximum pwr. at the desired frequency, and not at 3.5 and 7 MHz in this example. A balanced push-push doubler (diode or transistor) is well suited to the application (see **Solid State Design**).

I can't recommend too strongly the use of shielding around the VFO circuit. Double-sided PC board material works well for homemade shield boxes. An enclosed VFO module will be more stable since temperature changes will not be pronounced, and stray RF from the transmitter will not be apt to get into the VFO to cause errat-ic operation.

2.6 Practical 40-Meter VFO

The circuit in Fig. 2-4 is one I have used many times for operation on 1.8, 3.5, 5, 7 and 10.1 MHz. It has been reliable, easy to build and quite stable. Drift, after a 10-minute warmup at 7 MHz, should not exceed 100 Hz for any one-hour period, assuming a relatively constant ambient temperature. Although this VFO is designed for 7-MHz use, the component values can be altered for opreration on other frequencies by determining the reactance values of the critical elements, then calculating new values for the L and C parts. This will provide a close approximation of the values needed, but some final "trimming" will be needed to obtain the desired tuning range.

A series-tuned Colpitts oscillator is used at Q1, for the reasons given in section 2.5 of this chapter. Main-tuning capacitor C3 will work best, in terms of stability, if it has a bearing at each end of the rotor shaft. Select a smooth-running variable if you wish to avoid erratic tuning. A vernier-drive mechanism for C3 will aid smooth tuning, and it will enable you to plot a calibration chart versus the dial numbers.

Q2 is a source follower. The gain is 0.9. Therefore, Q3 is needed to amplify the VFO signal to a usable level. Q3 operates linearly in Class A. This minimizes harmonic generation. Additional suppression of harmonic currents is offered by the pi-network tank circuit of Q3. It is designed to provide an impedance transformation between Q3 and a 50-ohm load. The network has a loaded Q of 4. The 3.9K-ohm swamping resistor across L2 is used to broaden the response of the tuned circuit. It also prevents Q3 from self-oscillating when the load is other than 50 ohms.

Double-sided PC board is not recommended for this circuit. The copper conductor in combination with the PC-board insulating material, forms many small, unwanted capacitors. They are very temperature-sensitive, which gives rise to VFO drift. Therefore, you will fare better when using single-sided PC boards. The board should be mounted on the main chassis in a rigid manner. This will minimize frequency shifts caused by vibration and flexing of the circuit board.

A short, fairly stiff connecting lead is needed between C3 and L1. The C3 rotor must be grounded not only to the front panel and chassis, but also to the ground bus of the VFO PC board.

L1 should not only be coated with high-quality coil cement, it needs to be mounted securely to the PC board. I have found that placing a generous dab of clear RTV or silicone sealant between the toroidal coil (L1) and the PC board affixes the coil securely.

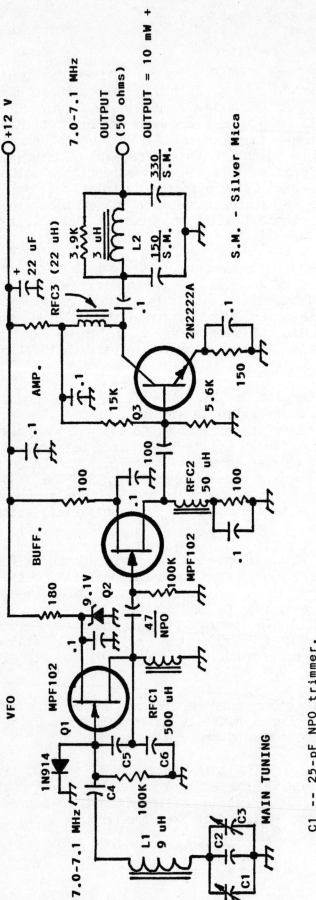

C1 -- 25-pF NPO trimmer.
C2 -- 100-pF NPO ceramic.
C3 -- 10-pF air variable (double bearing).
C4 -- 150-pF NPO ceramic.
C5, C6 -- 680-pF NPO ceramic.
L1 -- 43 turns no. 26 enam. on T68-6 (yellow) toroid.
      Apply two coats of coil cement.
L2 -- 24 turns no. 26 enam. wire on T50-2 toroid (red).
RFC1, RFC2, RFC3 -- Miniature iron-core RF choke.

Fig. 2-4

2.7 Poor Ham's QRP Rig

The budget special of Fig. 2-5 should be within the means of any ham's wallet. Additionally, the circuit is simple and easy to build. Three "generic" 2N2222A transistors comprise the RF part of the circuit. Q1 operates as a crystal oscillator, and Q2/Q3 function in parallel as a Class C amplifier. With 2N2222As selling between 3/$1 and 5/$1 on the surplus market, a dollar will pay for your RF devices while allowing a couple of spares to be set aside for future use.

Y1 operates in the fundamental mode from 80 through 20 meters. Overtone (3rd) crystals must be used for 15, 12 and 10 meters. Power output will be slightly lower on the three upper bands than from 80 through 20 meters. Also, chirp may be a problem on 15, 12 and 10 meters. If so, the oscillator (Q1) should not be keyed. Rather, the power amplifier (Q2/Q3) should be keyed. This will require a huskier keying transistor (Q4) to handle the additional dc current of the PA. A 2N4036 or 2N4037 is suggested for Q4. An equivalent PNP transistor may be used in place of a 2N4036.

The keying transistor, Q4, conducts when the key is closed, thereby routing dc to Q1. When the key is open, Q4 cuts off to stop the flow of dc. The RC network in the base leg of Q4 shapes the CW characters to prevent clicks. Softer keying will result if a larger capacitance is used in place of the 0.47-uF capacitor indicated. A hand key, bug or electronic keyer can be used with Q4. The keyer must be set for **positive** keying circuits.

Power output from the Poor Ham's QRP Rig should be approximately 1/2 watt from 80 through 20 meters. Greater power output may be noted, with up to 1 watt being developed. This will depend on the actual gain of the 2N2222As selected, and will be dependent also on the crystal activity. C2 can be detuned to reduce the power if this occurs, since 1 watt of output can cause excessive heating of Q2 and Q3. Heat sinks can be added to the PA transistor bodies to permit higher power levels, up to 3/4 watt. A 5.6-ohm resistor is used in the emitter lead of each PA transistor to prevent one transistor from "hogging" power, if one device has more gain than the other. The resistors also place Q2 and Q3 farther into the Class C region, which improves the efficiency.

A switch may be added to permit multifrequency operation. Several crystals can be used to replace Y1 if this is done. For use from 80 through 20 meters, you may want to try the VXO arrangement of Fig. 2-2 (L1 and C3 of that Fig.). VXO operation will not be feasible when using overtone crystals. Table 2-1 lists the parts values for the various bands of operation.

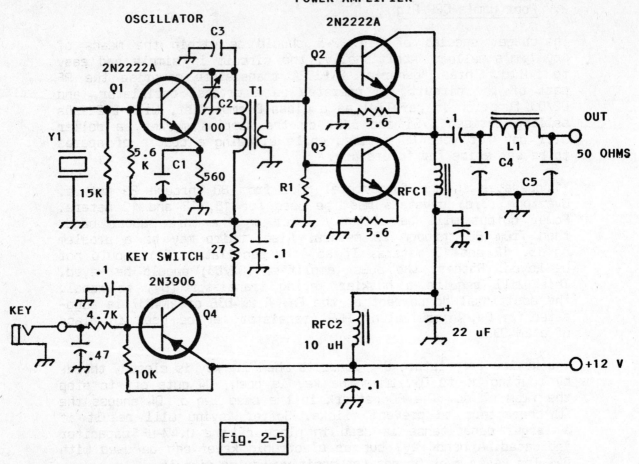

OSCILLATOR — POWER AMPLIFIER — KEY SWITCH

Fig. 2-5

C2 -- Mica compression trimmer, 100 pF.
L1 -- (80M) 20T no. 26 enam. on T50-2 toroid: (40M) 14T no. 24 on T50-2;
    (30M) 12T no. 22 on T50-2; (20M) 12T no. 22 on T50-6; (15M) 10T no.
    22 on T50-6; (12M) 9T no. 22 on T50-6; (10M) 8T no. 22 on T50-6.
T1 -- (80M) 52T no. 30 enam. on T50-2, sec. = 10T; (40M) 26T no. 28 on
    T50-2, sec. = 5T; (30M) 18T no. 26 on T50-2, sec. = 3T; (20M) 19T
    no. 26 on T50-6, sec. = 4T; (15M) 13T no. 22 on T50-6, sec. = 3T.
    (12M) 11T no. 22 on T50-6, sec. = 2T; (10M) 10T no. 22 on T50-6,
    sec. = 2T.

TABLE 2-1

	80M	40M	30M	20M	15M	12M	10M
C1 (pF)	1000	470	470	270	39	33	27
C3 (pF)	100	100	100	56	0	0	0
C4 (pF)	1000	560	560	270	200	180	150
C5 (pF)	1800	820	600	470	300	270	220
R1 ohms	47	47	47	33	27	27	22
RFC1 uH	25	15	15	10	10	8	8
Y1 (mode)	fund.	fund.	fund.	fund.	OT	OT	OT

2.8 QSK 1-Watter for 20 M

Operation with a single crystal can be too restrictive for other than casual QRPing, especially in those bands where QRM is ever-present. A VXO provides freedom from being "rockbound" on one frequency. Fig. 2-6 shows a 20-M CW QRP transmitter that has six preset channels for the Q1 VXO. S1 selects the channels. We may substitute variable capacitor C1 for S1 and the related capacitors. This will give continuous frequency coverage over a spread of roughly 10 kHz.

Q2 operates as a class-A buffer. It is keyed along with Q1 by means of keying transistor Q4 -- a PNP switch. Q2 is a broadband amplifier by virtue of T1. The power amplifier, Q3, is also a class-A broadband amplifier, but the output of Q3 contains a 5-element low-pass harmonic filter, FL1.

D1 has been included to protect Q3 from damage when the load on the transmitter is other than 50 ohms. A large mismatch can cause excessive peak voltage at the collector of Q3, and this can destroy the transistor. Zener-diode D1 clamps the peak posit-ive voltage at 36, thereby protecting the transistor. It does not conduct during normal operation, since the peak collector-voltage is twice the supply voltage, or 24.

QSK (full break in) operation is possible by the addition of D2, D3 and L5. A portion (small) of the transmitter power is lost when the two diodes conduct. They act as switches that clip the positive and minus RF-voltage peaks, thereby shorting the line to the receiver antenna jack via J3. When the key is up, the diodes do not conduct, which allows the signal from the ant-enna to pass through the 27-pF capacitor and L5, thereby effect-ively connecting the antenna to the receiver. L5 has the same reactance as the 27-pF coupling capacitor. This forms a series-resonant circuit at the operating frequency, which helps to min-imize signal loss on receive. The diodes alone would result in a signal loss of some 6 to 10 dB. The series circuit shown in Fig. 2-6 was borrowed from a QRP transmitter design by W7ZOI.

Power output from this transmitter will be between 3/4 and 1 watt. The circuit can be used on other bands by changing the feedback capacitors at Q1 (47 pF), the value of L1, and the con-stants of FL1, the receiver sampling capacitor and L5. Values for FL1 can be taken from the normalized filter tables in the transmitting chapter of the **ARRL Handbook**. L5 and the related sampling capacitor have a reactance of 400 ohms. This data will enable you to calculate the inductance and capacitance values for other frequencies.

Keyed-waveform shaping is provided by the RC network at the base of Q4. Softer keying can be had by increasing the value of the 0.47-uF input capacitor at J1.

31

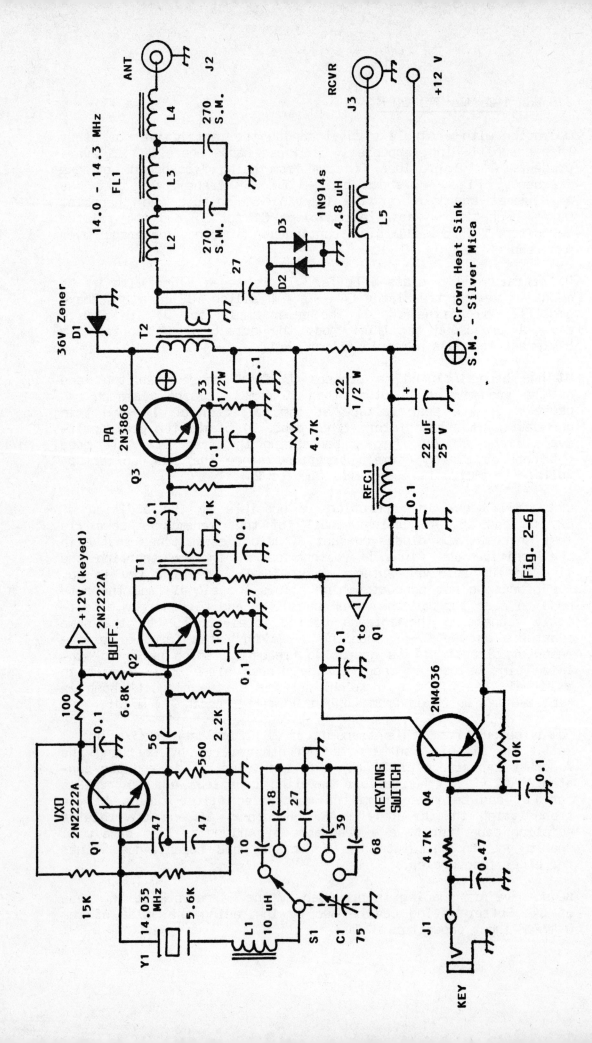

Fig. 2-6

As is the case with all RF circuits, the lead lengths for the transmitter of Fig. 2-6 should be short and direct to prevent self-oscillations and poor efficiency caused by unwanted impedances in the signal path. If instability should be observed, try bridging a resistance across the primary of T1 or T2. Start with 4.7K and lower. Use the largest resistance that will stop the self-oscillation, since the parallel resistor will consume part of the RF power.

Data for the coils and transformers used in Fig. 2-6 is: L1 - 42 turns of no. 26 enam. wire on an Amidon T68-2 toroid; L2, L4 - 10 turns of no. 24 enam. wire on a T50-6 toroid; L3 - 14 turns of no. 24 enam. wire on a T50-6 toroid; L5 - 30 turns of no. 26 enam. wire on a T50-2 toroid; RFC1 - 10 turns of no. 24 enam. wire on an Amidon FT50-43 ferrite toroid; T1 - 15 turns (pri.) of no. 26 enam. wire on an FT37-43 ferrite toroid. Sec. has 5 turns; T2 - 10 turns (pri.) of no. 24 enam. wire on an FT50-43 ferrite toroid. Sec. has 7 turns. Y1 should be an AT-cut fundamental crystal in an HC-6/U holder, 30 pF load capacitance. Select a crystal that is ground for the highest desired operating frequency. As series-connected VXO capacitance is added (S1 or C1, Fig. 2-6), the frequency will become lower. Keep all stray capacitance in the input (base of Q1, Y1 and S1) section of the VXO minimized to allow the maximum frequency swing of the crystal.

A VFO may be used with the transmitter in Fig. 2-6 by converting Q1 to a straight class-A amplifier and feeding the VFO signal to the base of Q1. Some means of offsetting the VFO frequency will be required for QSK operation (see Fig. 2-3C).

2.9 Boots for the 1-Watter

We may have an occasion to desire 8 or 10 watts of power output for QRP work, but generally a 1-W rig and a good antenna will be more fun, and it will be in keeping with the true spirit of QRP operation. However, I would be remiss if I did not describe some type of "afterburner" for the one-watt transmitter of Fig. 2-6. Most CB power transistors are ideal for HF-band QRP work. But, a number of devices that have been designed for hi-fi audio service have fT ratings up to and beyond 50 MHz. A large number of these power transistors can provide good performance from 160 through 20 meters, and the cost per device may be as low as 50 cents on the surplus market. If an audio power transistor is used, select one that has an fT at least five times higher than the intended operating frequency of your transmitter.

The amplifier in Fig. 2-7 contains two CB transistors by Motorola. A power output of 8 watts is typical, but one can obtain 10 watts by increasing the drive. Since the amplifier is broadband, class C, only the filter needs to be changed for use on a specific band. You may, therefore, tailor it for your needs.

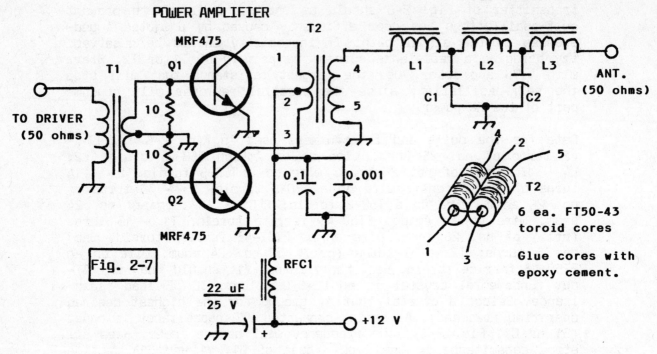

POWER AMPLIFIER

FL1 (TABLE 2-3)

Fig. 2-7

6 ea. FT50-43 toroid cores

Glue cores with epoxy cement.

T1 has a turns ratio of 2.2:1 for transforming 50 ohms to 10 ohms. The primary has 12 turns of no. 24 enam. wire on an Amidon FT50-43 toroid core (mu = 850). The secondary has 5 turns, center tapped. T2 consists of stacked FT50-43 cores (6) arranged as shown in the inset drawing. The collector-to-collector impedance of Q1 and Q2 is 36 ohms. The T2 primary has one turn (U-shaped) of no. 20 insulated wire passed through the rows or cores. The center of the loop is tapped to provide the primary center connection (no. 2). A 2-turn winding is looped through the cores for the transformer secondary winding. Use no. 22 insulated hookup wire. For use from 1.8 to 7.0 MHz, use two primary turns and three secondary turns to ensure ample winding inductance.

RFC1 consists of 10 turns of no. 22 enam. wire on an FT50-43 toroid core. C1 and C2 are silver-mica capacitors. L1, L2 and L3 are T68-2 toroids for 3.5-10.1 MHz. Use T68-6 toroids for 20 through 10 meters. Values for FL1 can be taken from the filter tables in the transmitting chapter of recent **ARRL Handbooks**. Winding data for the toroid cores is available in the Amidon catalog.

Heat sinks must be used at Q1 and Q2 of Fig. 2-7. They can be homemade units fashioned from no. 16-gauge aluminum sheet. Each sink is U-shaped, measuring 1-1/2 x 1-1/2 x 1-1/2 inches. The tabs on Q1 and Q2 are common to the collectors, so you will need to insulate the transistors from the sinks, or the sinks from circuit ground. Apply silicone grease between surfaces.

2.10 Curing Instability

The most common bug-a-boo encountered by those of us who build QRP transmitters is instability. Self-oscillations may occur from the audio frequencies through UHF, even though we use care in layout and assembly of a new circuit. Some oscillations may be so strong in RF power stages that we can hear the transistors "scream!" I've actually seen a purple glow through the ceramic headers of RF power transistors during strong oscillation periods.

Fig. 2-8 shows a typical two-stage RF amplifier that we may have to deal with. Self-oscillations can often be detected by using a dip meter in the absorption mode, then sampling the various tuned circuits to look for indications on the meter. Tuning from VLF through VHF with receivers will often detect self-oscillation that is otherwise not observed. We may find three oscillation frequencies in a bad situation -- VLF, VHF and HF, all occurring at once! This is because a transistor with a high fT has incredible gain at some very low frequency, and gain encourages instability. The gain of a given transistor doubles with each octave lower, at least in theory. This means that VHF and UHF transistors can become quite unruly at HF and lower.

Fig. 2-8 shows four ferrite beads (Z1-Z4) that can be added, as needed, to suppress or damp VHF and UHF parasitics. Beads with a 125 or 850 permeability are generally used. The bead shown at Z4 is meant more for killing the Q of RFC1 than it is to damp VHF oscillations. It is more likely to prevent self-oscillations in the HF range. Alternatively, R2 (1K to 10K, typically) may be used to lower the Q of RFC1.

C1 may be made smaller than normal to reduce the gain of Q1. This will reduce the power output accordingly. R3, R4, C2, C3 and C6 serve as decoupling networks to keep the RF energy from one stage away from the other stage, via the +V line. Various capacitor values are shown to ensure effective bypassing from MF through UHF. C4, C5 and RFC2 (5-10 uH) form another decoupling network for use in stubborn cases of instability. R1 will vary in value from 10 to 47 ohms in most cases. It loads the transformer secondary winding to aid stability. The lower the value of R1 the lower the driving power to Q2, since the resistor will permit power to be dissipated within it. Use the highest resistor value that will provide stability.

All PC-board foils should be short and direct in RF circuits. They should also be as wide as practicable. Short, wide foils are not as inductive as narrow, longer ones. These parasitic inductances form tuned circuits that encourage VHF and UHF oscillations. The pigtails on transistors, resistors and bypass capacitors must also be as short as practicable.

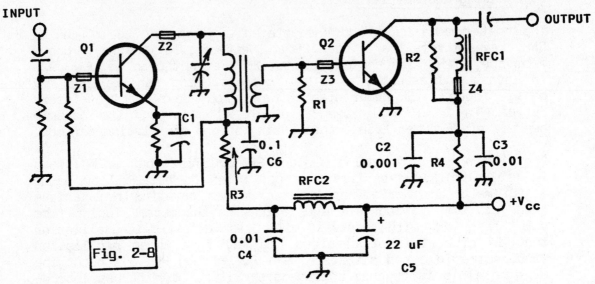

Fig. 2-8

2.11 MOS Power FETs for RF Amplifiers

Metal-oxide silicon (MOS) power FETs are abundant today, and they offer some distinct advantages over bipolar power transistors. Power FETs are not subject to thermal runaway, which can destroy a transistor almost immediately. Also, the power FET can provide higher efficiency than a bipolar transistor in a given class of service. The class-C bipolar device yields between 50 and 60 percent efficiency in a typical case, whereas the power FET has delivered measured efficiencies as great as 90% in narrow-band RF amplifier use. I have measured the efficiency of a single-ended class-C power amplifier at 85% in a 40-meter tuned amplifier. Another advantage of the FET amplifier is that the input impedance is high -- a megohm or greater -- if it is not dragged down by addition of external loading. This high input Z makes it easy to drive (low power excitation). Fig. 2-9 shows a simple circuit that we will use for discussion purposes.

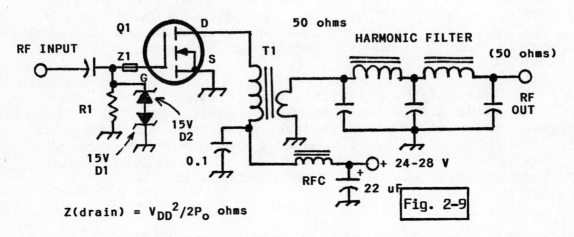

$$Z(drain) = V_{DD}^2/2P_o \text{ ohms}$$

Fig. 2-9

35

First, it is important to understand that most power FETs, irrespective of the application for which they are manufactured, will work at HF (3.5-29 MHz), and will often perform well as high as 2 meters. This is because in order for the device to qualify as a power FET, it must have an internal structure that permits fast switching (low drain-source resistance). Some power FETs, especially the high-power ones intended for dc switching, have high input and output capacitances. This feature makes them difficult to work with at the higher frequencies. But, most of the QRP-level FETs (10 W or less dissipation) are entirely suitable for our transmitters below 30 MHz.

The shortcomings of power FETs are few, but I should mention that they are prone to VHF parasitic oscillation. Z1 of Fig. 2-9 should be used as a matter of design practice to damp such oscillations. One or two 850-mu ferrite beads at the gate of Q1 will suffice. The gate impedance can be determined by way of R1. Its value sets the input Z of the amplifier. Q1 depends on pk-pk RF voltage swing from gate to source, so the higher the value of R1 the easier it becomes to turn on the FET. However, R1 values in excess of, say, 1000 ohms encourage amplifier instability. I like to keep the value below 300 ohms in my circuits. A 50-ohm resistor at R1 provides a common impedance for most exciters to look into.

The pk-pk voltage at the gate of a power FET should not exceed approximately 35 V. Values beyond that limit will puncture the gate insulation and destroy the transistor. If you are in doubt about the pk-pk voltage available from your exciter, add Zener diodes D1 and D2 as protective devices. They will limit the positive and negative voltage peaks to 15. Addition of the diodes will, however, add shunt capacitance at the gate, and this must be taken into account when designing the circuit.

Power FETs like high drain-source voltage. They are designed to be operated from a 24-V supply, or greater. They will produce some power at 12 V (roughly 0.25 the power at 28 V), but they saturate easily at reduced drain-source voltage, and the efficiency at lower operating voltages deteriorates. We should try to design for a 24-V power supply if we plan to use power FETs.

Linear operation is excellent with power FETs. Forward (plus) bias is applied to the gate. Normally, +1 V to +3 V is required to bias a power FET into the class-B or class-AB region. A resistive divider connected to the drain-supply line will suffice.

Another advantage of the power FET is that the input and output capacitances do not change with the driving-power level, as they do with bipolar transistors. Therefore, designing a feedback network for linear amplifiers is simple, and it will provide uniform feedback over a wide frequency range.

2.12 **Transmitter Design Tips**

There are some subtle design steps that we need to be aware of when planning a QRP transmitter. Notable among them is the need for us to take a reverse approach to power distribution with vacuum tubes: The usual practice for tube circuits is start with the oscillator, then select a following stage that can be driven sufficiently by the oscillator. Next, we move to the driver and hope for enough output power to properly excite the PA tube of our choice. The game is played differently with transistors: First, we must select a desired output power from the transmitter, then choose a transistor that can fulfill that need. Our next decision is to pick a driver that can supply the needed drive to ensure that the PA delivers its rated output. We must look at the specifications for the transistors. The two important device characteristics are fT and gain. We are interested in the gain (in dB) at our chosen operating frequency. Once the gain is known, along with the desired transmitter output power, we can determine how much driving power is required. Thus, if we desired a 10-W transmitter output power, and if the PA device was rated at 10 dB of gain, our required driving power would be 1 W (Gain = 10 log P1/P2 dB). The same reasoning will apply when planning the stage preceeding the driver, and so on. An example of this situation is shown in the block diagram of Fig. 2-10A. There must be some allowance for power loss in the coupling circuits between stages (just as with tubes), so always plan to have slightly more driving power than is required at the base of the transistor being driven. Keep in mind that transistor gain increases as the operating frequency is lowered, as mentioned earlier in this chapter.

Broadband circuits represent a tradeoff between stage gain and bandwidth. That is, a narrow-band amplifier (Fig. 2-10B) will have greater gain than an untuned, broadband amplifier (Fig. 2-10C). A QRP transmitter that uses tuned stages throughout, requires fewer stages to obtain a specified transmitter output power, compared to a broadband transmitter. But, the advantage of broadband circuits is that we eliminate complicated switching in multiband rigs, and the broadband circuit will have fewer parts. Another plus feature for broadband amplifiers is that they are less prone to self-oscillation. T1 of Fig. 2-10B and C is designed to provide an impedance match between Q1 and the following stage. This ensures maximum power transfer. The collector impedance is approximately $Vcc^2/2Po$, where Z is in ohms, V is in volts and P is in watts. Hence, if our output power were 5 watts and the supply voltage (Vcc) were 12, the impedance of the collector would be 144/10 = 14.4 ohms.

Calculating the base impedance of the following RF amplifier is not an easy matter. Most RF power amplifiers present an input impedance of less than 10 ohms. The higher the driving power

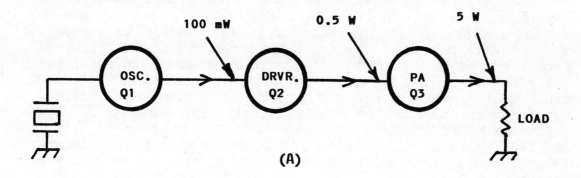

(A)

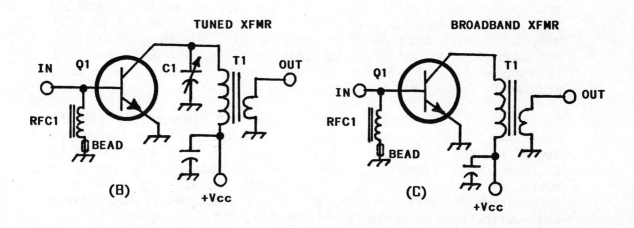

TUNED XFMR

BROADBAND XFMR

(B)

(C)

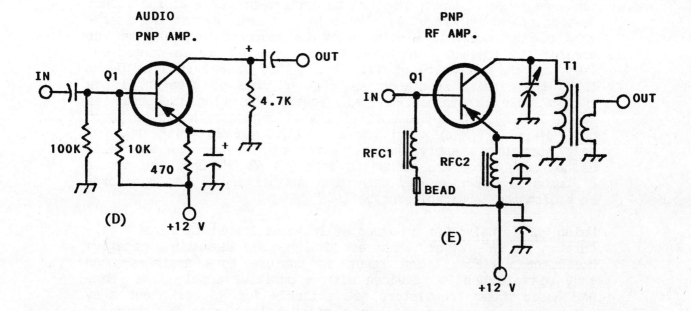

AUDIO
PNP AMP.

PNP
RF AMP.

(D)

(E)

Fig. 2-10

the lower the base impedance -- as low as 1 ohm in some instances. Therefore, I assume a 10-ohm base impedance, and wind the transformer accordingly. It then becomes an easy matter to remove one secondary turn at a time until I observe maximum outut power from the stage being driven. If the power drops as more turns are removed, you will be aware that a mismatch (and insufficient coupling) has occurred. Remember that the transformer turns ratio is the square root of the impedance ratio. For example, if we needed to match 40 ohms to 10 ohms, the Z ratio would be 4:1, but the voltage or turns ratio would be 2:1, and that determines the ratio of turns between the transformer primary and secondary windings.

The toroid core material for HF-band tuned transformers (Fig. 2-10B) should, for the most part, be powdered iron. The mix or recipe for the core is chosen for the best Q at the operating frequency. I suggest no. 2 (red) cores for use from 1.8 to 10.1 MHz, and no. 6 core material (yellow) for 14 through 50 MHz. The exception is when using toroids for VFO coils: No. 6 material is recommended for 160 through 30 meters, since it is a more stable mix than is the no. 2 material.

For use from 1.8 through 30 MHz, I use 850-permeability ferrite cores for broadband transformers. Ferrite cores with a permeability of 125 are my choice from 30 through 220 MHz, when designing broadband transformers. Lower values of permeability are also suitable for VHF use. The Amidon Assoc. catalog contains good information on this subject, as does **Ferromagnetic Core Design and Applications Handbook** (Prentice-Hall, Inc.), by W1FB.

Transformer Inductance: Broadband transformers must have sufficient reactance in their windings to perform properly at the lowest desired operating frequency. The rule of thumb is that the reactance of the smallest winding must be approximately 4 times or greater the impedance of the terminal to which it is connected. Thus, if the secondary of T1, Fig. 2-10C, looked into a 10-ohm load, the winding reactance would be 40 ohms or greater. I use the 4X rule. Therefore, if our lowest operating frequency is to be 3.5 MHz, the inductance of the T1 secondary would be based on L(uH) = XL/f(MHz) x 2pi, or L = 40/3.5 x 6.28 = 1.82 uH. Our next step is to apply the AL factor of the core, which tells us how many turns are needed to obtain 1.82 uH. Once the number of turns is known, we may then wind the primary of T1 in accordance with the required turns ratio.

Using PNP Transistors: A number of low-cost transistors are available in the PNP format. These are designed for use with a negative collector voltage, which tends to confuse some amateurs when they wish to use PNP devices with a positive supply line. Many PNP audio power transistors are suitable for RF work, and they can be used satisfactorily in a circuit that uses NPN devices.

Fig. 2-10D and E contains examples of PNP transistors that are used with a +12-V power supply. The circuit at D is an audio amplifier. Note that the collector is returned to ground through the 4.7K resistor. Operating voltage is applied to the emitter, and the smaller of the two base-bias resistors is returned to the emitter of Q1. This arrangement permits the mixing of NPN and PNP devices in a circuit that has but one power-supply polarity. If the power supply had a negative output bus, we could use NPN transistors by treating them in the same manner as the PNP device of Fig. 2-10D. A second example of a PNP amplifier and a +12-V supply is shown at E of Fig. 2-10. In this case we indicate the use of a PNP transistor in an RF power amplifier.

2.13 Harmonic Filtering

Spectral purity is as important at the QRP level as it is when using QRO (high power). Harmonic radiation becomes a more significant matter with transistors than with vacuum tubes. Not only is harmonic energy generated by envelope distortion (as with tubes), it is enhanced in the transistor by means of nonlinear changes in junction capacitance over the sine-wave cycle. It is not uncommon to find the second and third harmonics at the collector of a transistor amplifier only 10 dB below the desired peak-output power. Therefore, the harmonics from a poorly designed QRP transmitter can cause severe TVI, and they may result in unlawful signals outside the amateur frequencies. This relates to an earlier statement in this book, "QRP does not denote circuit simplicity."

There is no reason why our QRP rigs can't be as clean as commercial transmitters that must comply with FCC regulations about spectral purity. I strive to have all spurious energy at least 40 dB below peak output power. This is not hard to achieve.

Table 2-2 contains data for simple half-wave, low-pass harmonic filters. They are designed for a bilateral impedance of 50 ohms, with a loaded Q of 1. For QRP transmitters we may use 0.5-inch toroid cores for the inductors (T50). No. 2 (T50-2) cores are suitable up to 10.1 MHz. Yellow cores (T50-6) should be used from 14 to 30 MHz. The capacitor values listed are according to the design equation, and are not all of standard value. You may use parallel or series combinations of capacitors to obtain the exact values listed. However, the nearest standard value will usually provide adequate filter performance.

Table 2-3 lists component values for a five-element low-pass harmonic filter. This circuit offers better harmonic suppression than does the simple half-wave filter of Table 2-2. I use this one for power levels in excess of 1 watt.

TABLE 2-2

HALF-WAVE FILTER

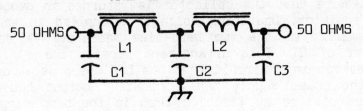

PART No.	BAND (METERS)							
	160	80	40	30	20	15	12	10
C1,C3 (pF)	1273	707	398	289	212	138	117	102
C2 (pF)	2547	1415	796	579	424	276	235	204
L1, L2 (uH)	3.18	1.77	0.99	0.72	0.53	0.34	0.29	0.25

This filter is designed for a QL (loaded Q) of 1. XC1, XC3 = 50 ohms. XC2 = 25 ohms. XL1, XL2 = 50 ohms. This is a bilateral filter and has a characteristic impedance of 50 ohms.

TABLE 2-3

5-ELEMENT FILTER

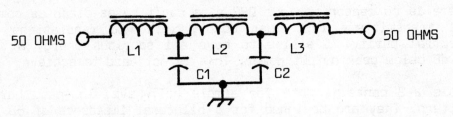

PART No.	BAND (METERS)							
	160	80	40	30	20	15	12	10
C1,C2 (pF)	1661	923	519	378	277	180	154	134
L1,L3 (uH)	2.4	1.33	0.75	0.55	0.40	0.26	0.22	0.19
L2 (uH)	5.0	2.78	1.56	1.14	0.84	0.54	0.46	0.40

This filter is designed for a ripple factor of 0.01, which results in an SWR of 1.10 between the amplifier and the antenna. Z = 50 ohms.

2.14 Adding Break-in Delay to the QRP Rig

Few QRP operators want to be bothered with manual switching when going from transmit to receive. Full break-in (QSK) may be your preference, and a practical example of how QSK may be added is shown in Fig. 2-6. However, you may opt for the kind of break-in format used in most HF-band transceivers, which is known as break-in delay. The circuit actuates almost instantly when the key is closed, but the recovery time is adjustable to provide a short or long delay before the receiver comes on during receive. Such a circuit is shown in Fig. 2-11. Q1 is a PNP dc switch. When the key is closed, Q1 is biased into conduction to place forward bias on the base of Q2. This turns on Q2, which in turn causes current to flow through the relay, K1, thereby closing the relay contacts. R1 is adjusted to provide the desired delay in K1 dropout. R1 and C1 establish the time constant for this function.

D1 through D3 are silicone high-speed switching diodes. D1 clamps on spikes that are created when the field in K1 collapses. This prevents transients from following the +12-V supply line, where they could cause damage to other parts of the circuit. D2 and D3 develop a reference voltage that ensures cutoff of Q2 when the key is up. Without these diodes the relay may not drop out during key-up periods. It depends on the quiescent current of the transistor used at Q2, plus the minimum hold-in current of the relay you select for K1. I have had good results with 12-V relays from Radio Shack. Any 12-V relay with a field-coil resistance of 400 to 1000 ohms should work OK at K1. I have actually used 24-V dc relays in this circuit, after loosening the spring tension sufficiently to permit them to pull in at 12 V, key down. C1 should be a tantalum capacitor for best results. Equivalent transistors may be used at Q1 and Q2 if the RCA units specified are not available.

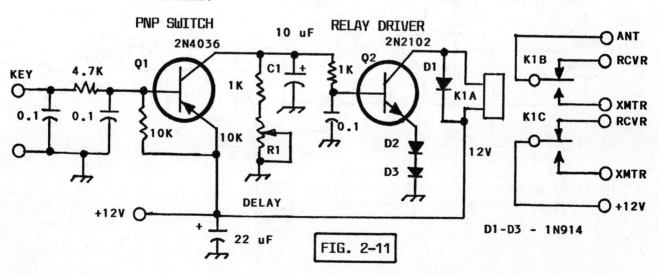

FIG. 2-11

41

CHAPTER 3

QRP ACCESSORY GEAR

There is little difference between the types of accessory equipment needed for QRP stations and QRO fixed-location gear. The major difference is that QRP accessories are smaller and less costly to build, such as SWR indicators and Transmatches. We will focus in this chapter on the most common of the "extras" that relate to QRP operation at home and afield.

3.1 AC Power Supplies

We discussed in the receiving chapter a problem with common-mode hum when using DC receivers with ac-operated dc power supplies. The cures for this problem are fairly simple and inexpensive, so it makes sense to design the ac-operated supply to include the necessary hum-reduction components. This will have no adverse effect on transmitter performance, and will make our power supply suitable for any QRP-related task.

Fig. 3-1 shows a circuit that fits the above description. Note the use of 0.01-uF bypass capacitors across the primary of T1. The capacitors should be rated at 1000 V to ensure leeway for line-voltage transients. C1 through C4 may be 100-V capacitors, but 600- or 1000-V units may be used also, if they are on hand. These capacitors bridge the diodes to prevent unwanted rectification of HF RF currents, but they do not affect the diode performance at the 60-Hz line frequency.

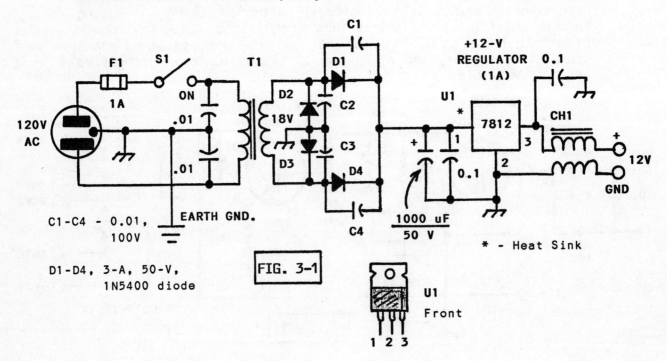

FIG. 3-1

Although 1-A diodes would be suitable for D1-D4, 3-A units will allow some safety factor in the interest of reliability. T1 is an 18-V, 2-A Radio Shack transformer (no. 273-1515). This, plus the other components specified, will enable the power supply to deliver 12 V, regulated, at 1-A maximum load current. A 1-A transformer may be used at T1, but it will be marginal in rating for dc current in excess of roughly 500 mA.

If you locate a surplus power transformer that is rated at 16 V, it will work OK in the circuit of Fig. 3-1 without any changes. A 24-V transformer may be used, but I don't recommend this. The higher voltage requires greater power dissipation in the regulator (U1), which will limit the available power-supply output current. The lower the T1 secondary voltage the cooler will be the regulator IC. A Radio Shack no. 276-1771 IC is used at U1. You may substitute a huskier IC at U1 without making circuit changes. This will provide some leeway in the power-supply ratings, and will add to the safety margin under full-load conditions.

CH1 of Fig. 3-1 is a bifilar choke that is mounted at the output terminals of the power supply, inside the cabinet. It consists of a two-wire parallel winding of 20 turns of no. 20 enamel wire on an Amidon Assoc. FT-114-43 ferrite toroid core. This choke will prevent RF signal energy from migrating to the power supply diodes via the 12-V power leads from the rig. The rectifier diodes are Radio Shack no. 276-1141 units.

U1 requires a heat sink to prevent shutdown or damage from excessive heat under high load current. A homemade sink fashioned from no. 16 gauge brass or aluminum is suggested. It may be a U-shaped heat sink with a dimension of 1-1/2 x 1-1/2 x 1-1/2 inches or larger.It should be insulated from ground, or the tab on U1 can be insulated from the heat sink by means of a mica insulator for a TO-220 transistor. If the insulator is used, be certain to spread a thin layer of silicone heat-transfer compound between the mating surfaces of the sink, regulator and   insulator.

3.2 SOLAR ELECTRIC POWER

I used bold-face capital letters for this heading, mainly to attract your attention to an ideal power source for QRP work. Photovoltaic power generation is becoming more popular as increased production is bringing down the cost of solar cells. Large solar panels are still expensive, especially those in the 1- and 1.5-A class, but low-current units are reasonable in cost, and are ideal for the QRP person.

A solar cell, irrespective of the current rating, generates roughly 0.5 V at peak, unoccluded sunlight. Power is generated within the cell when photons from the sun impinge on the cell surface.

Many cells must be connected in series to provide the necessary operating voltage for electronic equipment. Typically, there are 36 solar cells in series for a 12-V panel. Under no load, the solar panel will generate approximately 18 V of dc at peak sunlight. Some large solar-power systems contain "floating" regulators to limit the output voltage to a specific level. The floating regulator is one that consumes very little power during its operation.

If the solar-panel power is closely matched to the application for which it is used, a regulator is not needed. For example, too powerful a panel, when used with a low-capacity battery, can overcharge the battery and ruin it. But, even though we do not use a regulator with our system, we do need a gating diode in the power-output lead from the panel. D1 of Fig. 3-2 serves to isolate the solar panel from the buffer (battery) it charges. That is, the diode permits the passage of dc from the panel, but effectively divorces the battery from the panel during dark hours. If the diode were not present, the solar panel would discharge the battery when charging was not taking place. A Schottky diode, rated in excess of the output current of the panel, is best suited for the job, since it has a low barrier voltage. The diode barrier voltage must be subtracted from the available output voltage of the panel. A silicon rectifier diode will cause a voltage drop of approximately 0.7, which for practical purposes is acceptable for amateur work.

Although some moderately priced 100-mA solar panels are available from such vendors as Edmund Scientific Company, we may prefer to build a homemade unit. I purchased a sufficient number of surplus rectangular 100-mA cells (surplus) to build a compact solar generator for QRP work at the 1-W power-output level. Thin wires were soldered carefully to the rear surfaces of the cells to place them in series with one another. Photovoltaic cells are actually thin silicon junction diodes, so moisture and excessive heat can ruin them. Use a 25-W soldering iron, and don't allow the tip of the iron to linger!

I affixed the cells to a piece of stiff, white cardboard by means of foam pads that have adhesive material on both sides. They were purchased at a variety store. The completed panel was then installed in an 8 x 10-inch picture frame which had a glass, rather than plastic, front plate. A tube of automotive windshield sealant was used to waterproof the seams where the frame and the glass met. An aluminum L-bracket was screwed to the bottom of the picture frame. This provided a mounting plate that enabled me to attach the solar panel to a small camera tripod. This scheme makes it easy to tilt and rotate the panel toward the sun as it moves across the horizon. D1 of Fig. 3-2 was located on the rear outer surface of the picture frame.

I obtained the small solar cells from Poly-Paks in Lynn, MA, but individual cells have been offered in the Edmund Scientific catalog also. My homemade solar panel was used to keep a bank of AA-size NiCd cells charged (12-V at 400 mA). I used the battery pack to operate an HW-8 QRP transceiver. You may be wondering what happens when the sun is obscured by clouds. Well, the solar panel will still deliver small charging currents, which effectively makes it a trickle charger. If flourescent lighting is used nearby, you may charge the battery pack (slowly) by locating the panel directly under the light fixture. The safe way to deal with the rainy-weather problem is to carry two NiCd packs. One can be trickle charging while the other unit is in use.

Solar-electric power is almost made to order for QRP operators. It falls into place with the general "ecology" of low-power operation. What could be more convenient a power source for campers, boaters and those who do back-packing? I use a 600-mA solar panel in my 14-foot power boat to keep the 12-V battery charged, and this is essential when I am on wilderness lakes for several days at a time. I also use the solar panel to charge the batteries in my White's 6000-D metal detector when I am camping.

SOLAR-ELECTRIC PANEL

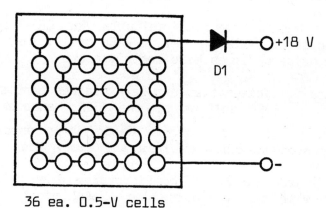

36 ea. 0.5-V cells

Fig. 3-2

3.3 A 12.5-V NiCd Battery Pack

Although we may use a wet-cell battery to power our QRP gear, such as a 12-V motorcycle battery, the NiCd pack seems to enjoy greater popularity for portable use. At least there is no dangerous acid to spill from a NiCd battery! Some hams use 6-V dry batteries (two in series) that are used with lantern-type flashlights. The shortcoming is that they are expensive, and they can't be recharged. My preference is for battery packs made from

10 NiCd cells, size AA or C. The AA-size cells can be found on the surplus market (new units) for as little as $1 at times. These cells (10 each) can be connected in series to provide 12.5 V at 400 mA. The size-C and size-D cells cost more, but will provide a greater mA/hour rating.

I use a 50-mA charging rate when bringing these NiCd packs up from depletion, even though faster charging can be realized by boosting the charging current. The higher charging rates will shorten the battery life, so it's better to be patient and do the charging at 50 mA.

Care should be taken to prevent complete discharge of a NiCd cell. When this happens, some cells will reverse in polarity, which makes them unusable. Shorted cells can be "zapped" back to service on occasion by applying momentary high current to the plus and minus terminals. I use my variable dc bench supply for this purpose. I set the current control for 1 A, and adjust the output voltage level to approximately five times the battery or cell voltage. For a standard NiCd cell (1.25 V), I zap it with 5 V at 1 A by quickly touching the power-supply leads to the ends of the cell. After two or three zaps, many cells will recover, and they can be recharged. Zapped cells may short out later, but many additional hours of use may be possible before they can no longer be jolted back to a normal state.

Gell-Cell batteries are also suitable for QRP work. They may be recharged in a similar manner to NiCd cells. They are somewhat the same in price class as NiCd battery packs.

Battery Capacity: This matter can be explained best by a quotation taken from the 1984 edition of the **ARRL Handbook**, page 10-4:

> *The common rating of battery capacity in ampere hours, is a product of current drain and time. The symbol "C" is commonly used; C/10, for example, would be the current available for 10 hours continuously. The value of C changes with the discharge rate, and might be 110 at 2 amperes, but only 80 at 20 amperes.*

Therefore, if our 12.5-V, 400-mA/hr NiCd pack were used, it would be depleted after one hour if 400 mA were permitted to flow during that period. For intermittent transmitting (CW) at, say, 100 mA key down, the battery would last considerably longer than one hour, respective to its charge. However, the receiver current drain must be cranked into the equation as part of the long-term current drain. The CW duty cycle depends, of course, on the speed used when forming the Morse characters. Because of these consider-ations it is not a casual matter to calculate the battery charge life for a given QRP transmitter.

A circuit for a NiCd charger is provided in the **ARRL Handbook.** Radio Shack parts are used for the unit.

3.4 Antenna-Matching Devices

Most solid-state transmitters are designed to look into a 50-ohm load. It is necessary, therefore, that we provide a correct 50-ohm load for the transmitter. This can be done by means of a Transmatch (sometimes called an "antenna tuner"). The term "Transmatch" stands for <u>transmitter match</u>, which means the transmitter is matched to the feed line. If the network were located between the antenna feed point and the transmission line, then it would be correct to call it an <u>antenna tuner</u>.

Some Transmatches contain tapped coils. This poses a severe limitation under certain load conditions. That is, the coarse inductance choice leaves gaps in the inductance resolution, and a 1:1 match can't be achieved at all times. A variable inductor yields a complete set of LC ratios for matching, and it is the best scheme to adopt when possible. Unfortunately, commercial roller inductors are bulky and expensive -- not suited to QRP work. Therefore, we need to fabricate our own variable inductors from available materials.

An example of a low-cost QRP Transmatch is given in Fig. 3-3. The circuit is for a modified L network. Depending on load conditions, the connections to J1 and J2 may be reversed to obtain an SWR of 1:1. The heart of the network is L1, a homemade 5-uH variable inductor. The pictorial drawing shows how this assembly can be made. A ferrite rod with a permeability of 125 is pushed into and pulled out of a fixed-value 1.5-uH coil, L1. The inductance range will be approximately 1.5 to 5 uH. This coil is in the circuit at all times, irrespective of the settings of S1 and S2. When S1 is closed, L2 is in parallel with L1 and L3. This reduces the effective inductance of L1 to permit easy matching at 15, 12 and 10 meters. S2 should be set at the **MIN L** position when S1 is closed. With S2 in the **Max L** position, and with S1 open, the Transmatch is set up for 80-meter use. S2 is adjusted to the other tap positions for operation on 40, 30 and 20 meters. In each case, L1 is the adjustable element for inductance. C1 and C2 are miniature, single-section transistor-radio tuning capacitors. You may substitute 150-pF variable capacitors if you wish. A large, surplus slug-tuned coil form may be used for L1 if the core material is suitable for HF use.

A T-network Transmatch is shown in Fig. 3-4. It uses the same group of components as the circuit of Fig. 3-3. The series and parallel inductors, plus the switches, serve the same purposes as they do in the modified L network. The T network has a good matching range, and need not be reversed under certain load conditions, as does the L network. Ferrite rods may be obtained from Amidon Assoc. You may also use a rod from a BC-band loop antenna. These transistor-radio loops are often available as surplus.

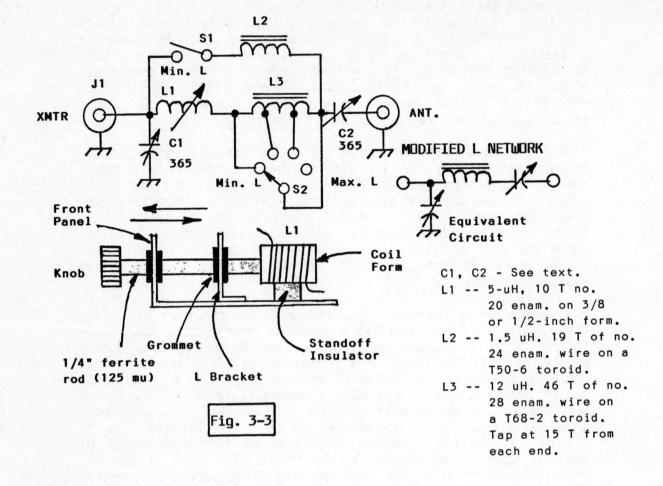

MODIFIED L NETWORK

Equivalent Circuit

C1, C2 - See text.
L1 -- 5-uH, 10 T no.
 20 enam. on 3/8
 or 1/2-inch form.
L2 -- 1.5 uH. 19 T of no.
 24 enam. wire on a
 T50-6 toroid.
L3 -- 12 uH. 46 T of no.
 28 enam. wire on
 a T68-2 toroid.
 Tap at 15 T from
 each end.

Fig. 3-3

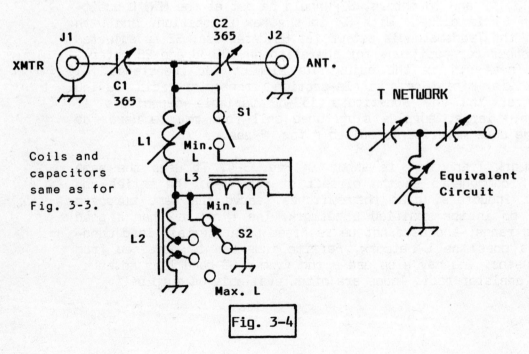

Coils and capacitors same as for Fig. 3-3.

T NETWORK

Equivalent Circuit

Fig. 3-4

3.5 SWR Indicators

A Transmatch is rather useless without an SWR-indicating instrument. Most commercial SWR or RF-power meters are not sensitive enough for QRP work, so once again we must build a unit for our low-power transmitters. Even though there are some commercial units that have a low-power scale (Daiwa CN-720 for one), the physical size is ludicrous for QRP stations! But, homemade SWR indicators are inexpensive, and they can be made very compact.

Fig. 3-5 contains the circuit for a sensitive SWR bridge. This circuit is a spinoff of the excellent design introduced some years ago by Walter Bruene (pronounced "brine") of Collins Radio. It has a full-scale sensitivity of less than 1 watt, and is suitable for use from 1.8 to 29 MHz. T1 normally has a single lead passed through the center of the toroid core, and at QRO levels this equivalent of one turn provides ample RF-current sampling. Our circuit requires a 2-turn link as the primary, which increases the bridge sensitivity sufficiently for QRP work. Current in the secondary winding of T1 is rectified by D1 and D2 to provide a dc voltage that deflects the needle of M1.

R1 is the sensitivity control for the bridge. Power is applied to the load through the bridge with S1 in the **FWD** position. R1 is set for a full-scale reading at M1. S1 is then switched to the **REF** position and the Transmatch is adjusted for a zero reading on the meter. This corresponds to an SWR of 1.

C1 and C2 are used to balance the bridge after it is built. A 50-ohm resistive load is connected first to J2. C1 is adjusted for zero indication on M1 with S1 set for **REF**. After this is done, the load is attached at J1, and C2 is adjusted for zero reflected power. No further adjustment is required. M1 should be a microammeter for best low-power sensitivity. A 50-uA instrument would be better than the 100-uA meter specified, if you are willing to accept the higher cost of the more sensitive unit. But, many low-cost edgewise surplus hi-fi meters are OK for QRP SWR meters. Most have a full-scale sensitivity of 200 uA.

Fig. 3-6 shows a resistive bridge with superb low-power response. This circuit was popularized by the late George Grammer, W1DF.

This bridge, and the one in Fig. 3-5, require symmetrical layout and short leads for best results. Power is applied with S1 in the **CAL** position. R1 is adjusted for full-scale indication at M1. Next, S1 is set for **SWR**, and the Transmatch is adjusted for a zero indication at M1. Finally, S1 is set for **OPR**, which takes it out of the circuit. The 47- and 51-ohm resistors need to be noninductive, and must have twice the wattage of the RF power applied to the bridge. I use 2-W carbon-composition resistors for power levels up to 3 W. Momentary tests are OK at the 5-W level.

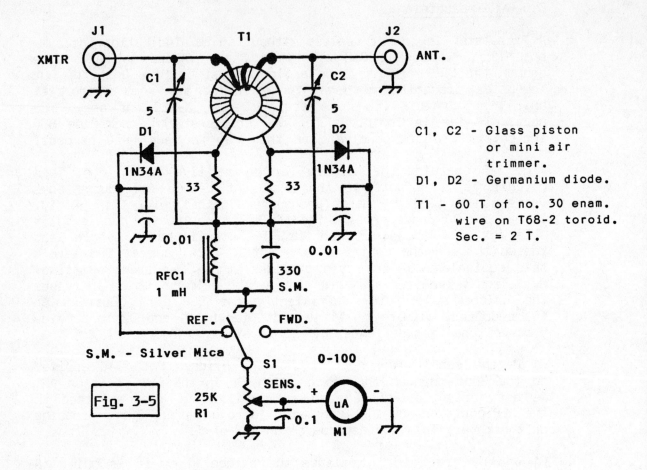

C1, C2 - Glass piston
          or mini air
          trimmer.

D1, D2 - Germanium diode.

T1 - 60 T of no. 30 enam.
     wire on T68-2 toroid.
     Sec. = 2 T.

Fig. 3-5

S.M. - Silver Mica

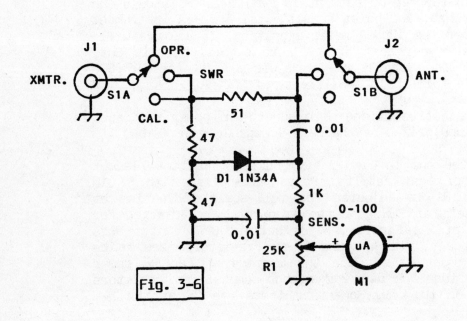

Fig. 3-6

3.6 100-kHz Marker

Most homemade QRP receiving equipment does not provide accurate frequency readout, owing to the use of analog dials. Therefore, it is almost essential to have a secondary frequency standard for keeping track of the band edges. This is especially important when operating a ham station outside the USA, where some foreign governments require a secondary standard when issuing an amateur license. Fig. 3-7 shows a 100-kHz oscillator that can be carried as an accessory unit for use with any receiver.

Q1 and Q2 operate as a multivibrator with the 100-kHz crystal in the feedback path. Trimmer C1 is adjusted to make the oscillator zero beat with WWV. Output from the marker oscillator is routed to the receiver antenna jack. The 27-pF coupling capacitor can be made lower in value, provided the markers are loud enough to be heard plainly on the various HF bands.

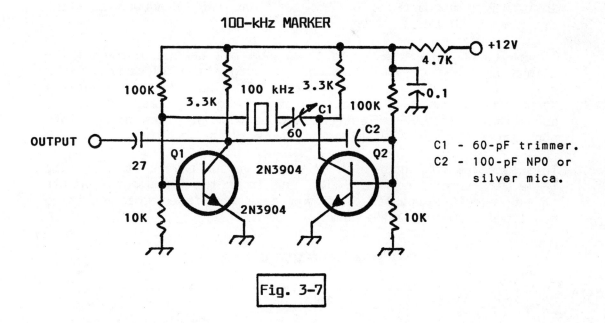

Fig. 3-7

3.7 Ladder Type Power Attenuator

If you're interested in the challenge of "miles per watt" when operating at QRP levels, you need a step attenuator that can be inserted in the 50-ohm feed line from your transmitter. If the attenuator is designed to provide 3-dB steps, it is an easy matter to calculate the incremental power reduction. For example, if the transmitter full-power output is 1 W, then a 3-dB step will reduce the power to your antenna by 0.5 W. Another 3-dB step will decrease the effective output power to 0.25 W, and so on. Philosophically, at least, this concept is in keeping with the FCC ruling that we use only the power necessary to maintain communications.

Fig. 3-8 shows a ladder type of attenuator that may be used for RF power levels up to 1.5 W, intermittent CW. The resistors are 2-W, carbon-composition units. Do not use wire-wound or other inductive resistors.

In the interest of keeping the resistor leads as short as possible, mount the resistors directly on the switch tabs. This will require a large rotary, wafer switch. Many of these are available at low cost from surplus-equipment vendors.

A more conventional step attenuator (one that uses separate slide or toggle switches for each step) may be used in place of the unit shown below. The isolation between the ends of the attenuator will be better (improved accuracy) if that type of construction is followed. It permits placing each attenuator section in a shield compartment of its own. The **ARRL Handbook** contains details for that kind of attenuator.

If you can't locate 2-W resistors, you may use parallel combinations of 1/2- or 1-W resistors to obtain the 18- and 300-ohm resistance values indicated in Fig. 3-8. Also, should you prefer steps other than 3 dB each, you may change the resistor values accordingly. The **ARRL Electronics Data Book** provides design info and tables of values for pi and T resistive attenuators.

This aspect of QRP operation (distance versus power) is a primary theme with such QRPers as W7ZOI, and is in the fundamental spirit of our specialty pastime. If you have not faced this exciting challenge, now may be the time!

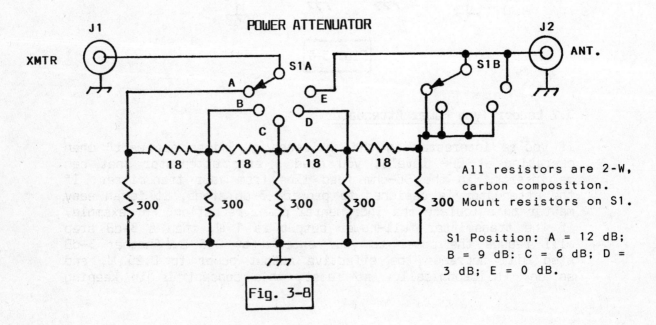

POWER ATTENUATOR

All resistors are 2-W, carbon composition. Mount resistors on S1.

S1 Position: A = 12 dB; B = 9 dB: C = 6 dB; D = 3 dB; E = 0 dB.

Fig. 3-8

3.8 RIT for QRP Transceivers

It is almost mandatory that we include an RIT (receiver increment-al tuning) circuit to a transceiver. Few transceivers have the same frequency offset between the transmit and receive modes, which makes an RIT circuit necessary for tuning the other stat-ion's signal for the desired beat or pitch.

Transceivers that contain DC receivers are especially in need of an RIT control, since there may be no offset between transmit and receive, owing to the VBFO/VFO being on the same frequency for both transmit and receive. Without offset of some type, we would find the the other station's signal at zero beat in our receiver, and hence no CW note to copy!

Fig. 3-9 illustrates schematically an excellent RIT circuit dev-eloped by Roy Lewallen, W7EL, for use in his high-performance 40-meter QRP transceiver (**QST** for August, 1980). I urge you to read the original article in the interest of learning how to obtain high performance in a very small package.

The VFO portion of the circuit in Fig. 3-9 is very stable because of the light coupling between the tuned circuit and Q1. Zero temperature coefficient capacitors are used in the frequency-critical part of the VFO, and this further aids the stability. W7EL tells in his **QST** article about how he treats or conditions his toroidal VFO coils for best stability. Two coatings of poly-styrene Q Dope, as discussed earlier in this book, can be used to hold the turns of L1 in place. The two-stage broadband buffer reduces VFO pulling when the transmitter part of the transceiver is keyed.

Q4 is a dc switch that conducts when the key is closed. During key closure, Q4 disables the RIT to ensure that the transmitter is on the desired frequency. When the key is up, R1 can be adjust-ed to move the VFO frequency above or below the transmit freq-uency during the receive period. D2 functions as a tuning diode when R1 is adjusted.

The general concept illustrated in Fig. 3-9 can be applied to other operating frequencies by modifying the critical constants. I have presented this circuit to serve mainly as a guidepost for those of you who enjoy building your own equipment.

As is true of any VFO, it is wise to place the circuit in its own shielded box to prevent fast changes in ambient temperature, and to prevent unwanted RF energy from entering the VFO circuit and causing erratic operation during transmit periods.

Fig. 3-9

NP0 CERAMIC

C1 - NP0 or air trimmer.
C2 - Miniature air variable.
D2 - 15-V, 400-mW Zener.
L1 - 3-uH inductor. 26 T no. 26 enam. on
     Amidon T44-6 (yellow) toroid. Tap
     7 T from ground end.
R1 - Linear-taper carbon control. Panel mount.
T1 - Broadband transformer. Pri. has 15 T of
     no. 28 enam. wire on Amidon BLN-43-2402
     balun core. Sec. uses 3 T.

RF OUT

+12 V

BUFFER

T1

27K

2N3904
Q3

0.1

180

0.1

2N3904
Q2

1K

VFO

+10 v Reg.

100

0.1

10K

2N4416
Q1

D1
1N914

2.7*

C1
5

1M

220*

30*

12*

C2
75

510*

MAIN TUNING

L1

7.0 - 7.15 MHz

15*

D2

1M

15V
0.5W

RIT

R1
20K

ZERO

S1

0.001

56K

18K

PNP SWITCH

2N3906

Q4

+10V
Reg.

100K

1N914
D3

10K

0.1

+12V

TO
KEY
LINE

3.9 Adding a Sidetone Generator

Not all keyers contain a sidetone oscillator for monitoring our CW sending. We may include a sidetone circuit in a transmitter or transceiver for monitoring in headphones or speakers. Many simple circuits are available, with the simplest one consisting of a unijunction transistor in a sawtooth oscillator. Twin-T transistor oscillators are sometimes used, but the purest tone comes from the phase-shift oscillator.

Another good circuit is the free-running multivibrator. A practical example of this circuit is shown in Fig. 3-10. Cross-coupled 2N3904s form a sidetone oscillator with more than ample output for most receiver audio channels. A series-connected 100K trimmer potentiometer is used between the oscillator and the input of the receiver audio amplifier. It permits setting the sidetone level for comfortable listening.

The oscillator frequency can be changed by altering the value of the feedback capacitors (0.01-uF units shown). The +12-V supply to the circuit of Fig. 3-10 is keyed by the control circuit (PNP switch) in the QRP transmitter. An example of this arrangement is given in Chapter 4, where a 40-meter transceiver is described.

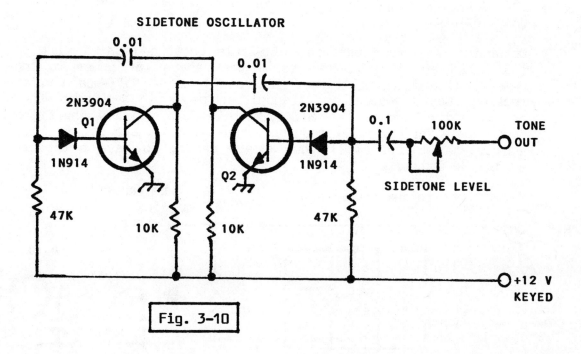

Fig. 3-10

3.10 Measuring RF Power

As we acknowledged earlier in this volume, RF wattmeters for the QRP level are scarce and bulky on the commercial market. Accurate measurements can be made with simple home-built test gear, such as the circuit depicted in Fig. 3-11.

Four 200-ohm, 2-W, 5% carbon-composition resistors are connected in parallel to form a 50-ohm, 8-W load. You may run a maximum of 5 W into this load continuously. Momentary key-down tests from 5 to 10 watts are possible without damage to the load resistors. If the resistors are immersed in a small metal can that has been filled with mineral oil, you may run 10 W into the load, continuously. The resistors should be mounted adjacent to each other, and the pigtails must be short and direct. This will minimize unwanted stray inductance, which can spoil the 50-ohm characteristic of the load, especially at the high end of the HF range. A good construction method is to sandwich the resistors between two PC-board end plates, then solder the resistor leads to the copper foils of the end plates.

An RF probe (see measurements chapter of the **ARRL Handbook**) is easy to build. It can be used with any VTVM or FET equivalent to provide RMS voltage readings across the dummy load. Alternatively, you may connect a 30-MHz (or higher) scope to the load test point in Fig. 3-11. This will give you pk-pk (peak-to-peak) RF voltage readings that can be converted to RMS values for power calculations.

Determine what your desired full-scale wattage reading will be (as indicated at M1), then apply that amount of power to the dummy load and adjust trimmer control R1 for a full-scale meter reading. Next, reduce the transmitter power in 1-W increments and note the readings on M1. From this data you may chart the power scale for the meter readings. You may eliminate the detector and related circuitry if you do not desire to have a direct-reading RF wattmeter.

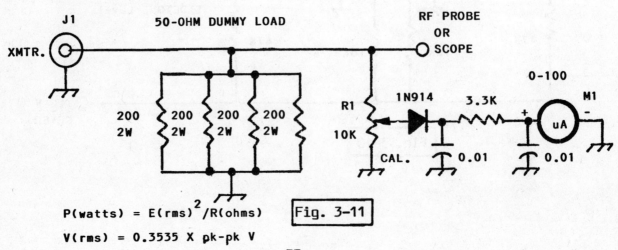

$$P(watts) = E(rms)^2/R(ohms)$$

Fig. 3-11

$$V(rms) = 0.3535 \times pk\text{-}pk\ V$$

CHAPTER 4

QRP TRANSCEIVING

Transceivers simplify QRP operating, and they are more compact than are "separates" (receiver and transmitter). However, we can combine a receiver with a transmitter in one cabinet to provide a "trans-receiver." The choice must depend on operating preferences and whether or not we want to become involved with designing and building a complex transceiver. The use of "separates" greatly simplifies the T-R switching technique, and it eliminates the need for a frequency-offset or RIT circuit. There is substantially more operating freedom when using a separate transmitter and receiver. One may listen many kHz away from the committed transmitting frequency, which is not possible with a transceiver that contains an RIT control. Fig. 4-1 shows a simplified block diagram of a direct-conversion transceiver.

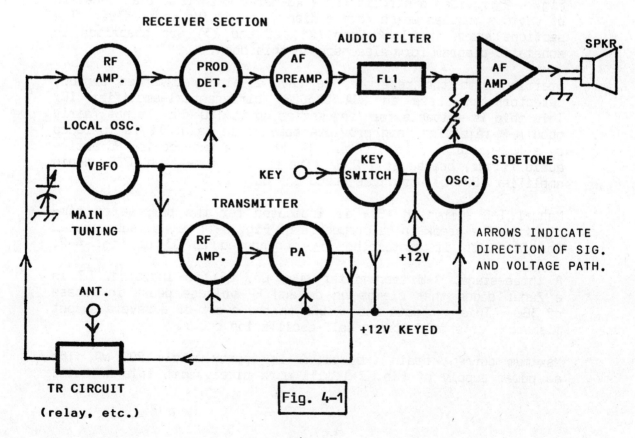

The VBFO operates on the same frequency for both transmit and receive, such as 3.5 to 3.8 MHz. The diagram does not show a frequency-offset circuit for shifting the transmitter 700 Hz below the receive frequency, but one needs to be included. Also, the T-R switching for the +12-V feed to the receiver section is not indicated.

The T-R circuit of Fig. 4-1 may be a solid-state QSK type, manual switching system, or a break-in delay scheme such as that of Fig. 2-11.

If we were to subscribe to the trans-receiver philosophy, it would still be necessary to include some type of T-R switching circuit for transferring the antenna and muting the receiver during transmit. But, the T-R circuit would not, in this case, be required to actuate the frequency-offset circuit, as would be the situation with a transceiver.

Another advantage in using separate units is that we may replace a transmitter or receiver section with a different one at any time, without disturbing the remaining module. This is an ideal arrangement for those of you who like to experiment.

4.1 A Practical 40-Meter DC Transceiver

Fig. 4-2 provides a circuit for a 40-meter mainframe that consists of various modules which form a direct-conversion transceiver. The sections shown in block form (Z1, Z2 and Z3) are described in schematic-diagram form elsewhere in this book.

Starting with the receiver, we have a singly balanced product detector that uses an RCA CA3028A differential-amplifier IC. This chip is suitable for frequencies up to 120 MHz. It has fairly good A-M rejection, and provides conversion gain. It is followed by a low-noise AF preamplifier, Q1. FL1 is a two-section RC active audio filter, peaked at 700 Hz. The popular two-stage W7ZOI audio amplifier (Q2, Q3) provides headphone output.

Manual T-R switching (S1) is indicated for the purpose of simplicity. The break-in delay module of Fig. 2-11 may be substituted for S1, with its actuating line connected to J3 of Fig. 4-2.

A three-stage, 1-W transmitter (Q4, Q5, Q6) is indicted. D2 is a Zener diode that clamps on dc and RF voltage peaks in excess of 36.   This protects the 2N3866 in the event of a severe output mismatch, or should strong self-oscillation occur.

Maximum current drain (key down) is approximately 200 mA. The ac power supply of Fig. 3-1 will work nicely with this circuit.

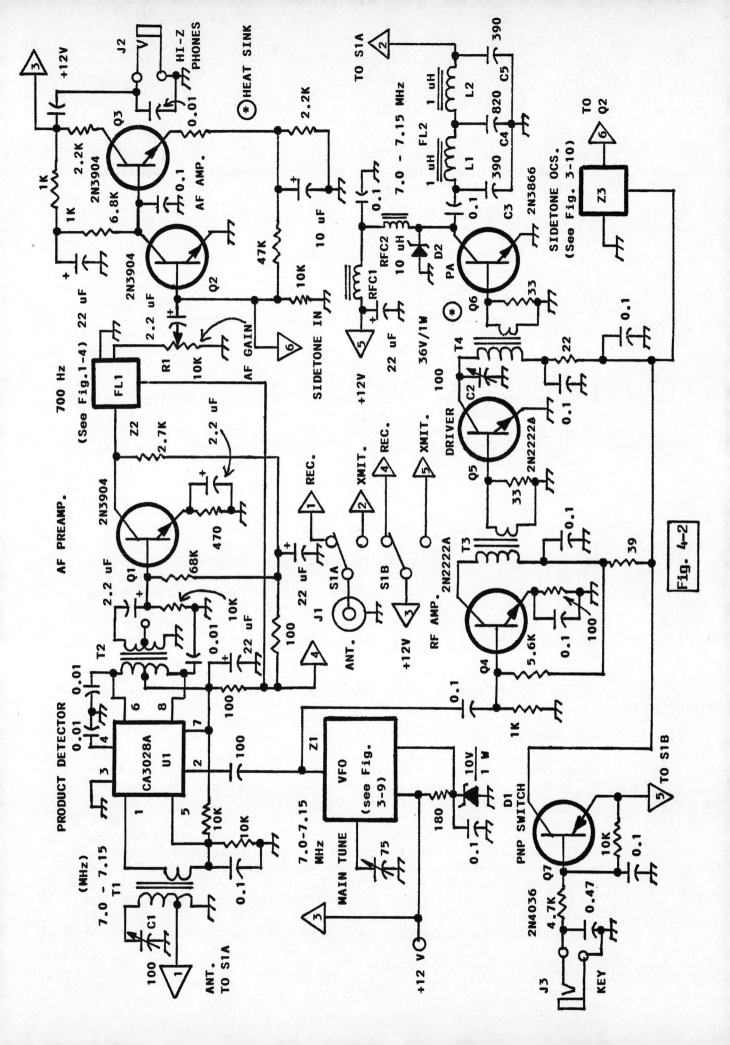

Fig. 4-2

If you have difficulty locating a CA3028A chip, you may use an RCA CA3046 transistor-array IC. A Motorola MC3346P may also be used. By adopting the CA3046 receiver circuit in **QST** for August 1985, p. 23, Fig. 4, you can eliminate the CA3028A and Q1 of Fig. 4-2. A PC board or parts kit for the module is available from A&A Engineering (see **QST** footnote).

Parts Information

C1, C2 -- 100-pF mica or ceramic trimmer.
C3, C4, C5 -- Silver mica or polystyrene.
D1, D2 -- Zener diode, 1 watt.
L1, L2 -- 14 turns of no. 24 enam. wire on Amidon T50-2 toroid.
R1 -- Audio-taper, carbon-composition, panel-mount control.
S1 -- SPDT toggle or wafer switch.
T1 -- 5.6-uH primary 33 turns of no. 28 enam. wire on Amidon T50-2 toroid core. Tap at 3 turns above ground end. Secondary winding has 10 turns of no. 28 enam. wire.
T2 -- Miniature audio transformer, 10,000-ohm center-tapped primary, 2000-ohm secondary (CT not used).
T3 -- Broadband transformer. 15 primary turns of no. 28 enam. wire on Amidon FT37-43 ferrite toroid. Secondary has 7 turns.
T4 -- Same as T1, except no primary tap. Secondary has 5 turns.
Z1, Z2, Z3 -- See circuit diagrams in chapters 1 and 3.

4.2 The Gutless Wonder Trans-Receiver

Earlier in the chapter we acknowledged the trans-receiver concept. It is therefore appropriate to include an example of such a "critter" in this part of the volume. Fig. 4-3 represents a degree of simplicity that can be acceptable for all but the most stringent of operating needs. I have dubbed the trans-receiver the "Gutless Wonder" because so few parts are involved.

Although the circuit is designed for 80-meter use, it can serve as the basis for a similar unit that you may wish to structure for use on 160, 40 or 30 meters. QSK operation is featured in the circuit of Fig. 4-3, and transmitter output power is between 3/4 and 1 watt.

Receiver: The antenna is routed to the product detector without RF amplification. An acceptable noise figure can be expected without a preamplifier if the receiver is used below 30 meters. I recommend a low-noise preamplifier at 20 meters and above. The product detector is followed by a low-noise audio amplifier (Q2). There is no audio filter included in the receiver. Therefore, selectivity for CW work will not be on par with that for the circuit of Fig. 4-2. You may add Z2 of Fig. 4-2 if you wish to include a selective circuit. It may be inserted between R1 and U1, the audio output stage. This IC boosts the AF energy to headphone level (8-ohm phones). A speaker may be used for copying

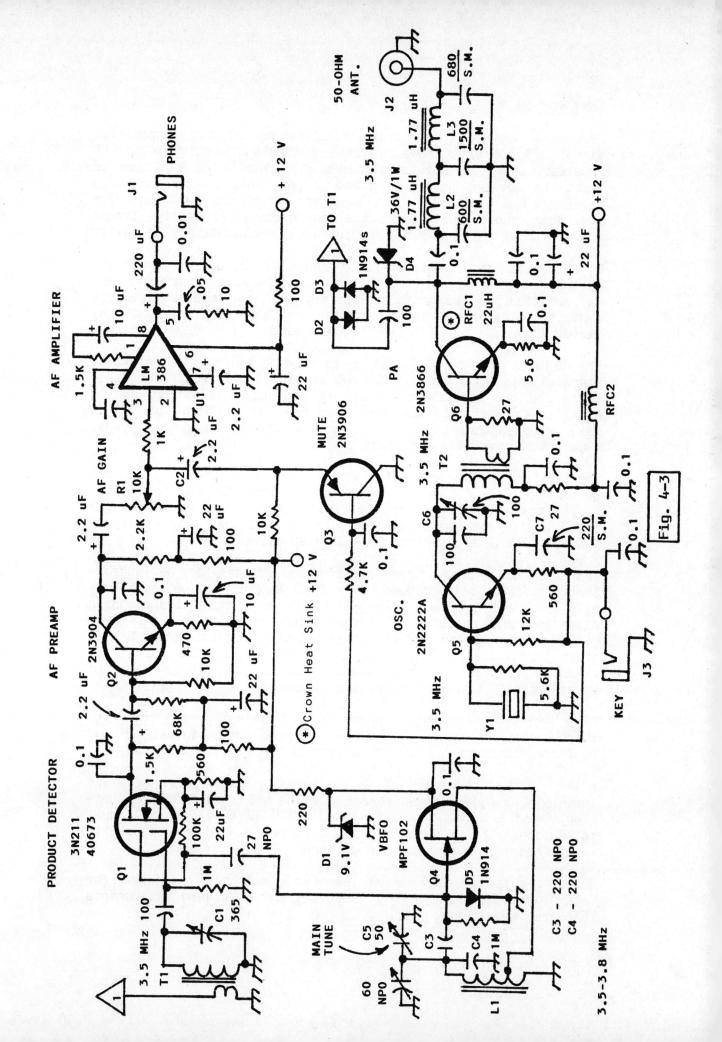

Fig. 4-3

loud signals.

Side-tone monitoring consists of listening to the transmitter signal. Q3 functions somewhat like a squelch circuit in an FM receiver. When the key is closed (J3), Q3 acts as a switch to bridge C2 between the AF line and ground. This lowers the audio level in the headphones. The value of C2 should be chosen for a sidetone audio level that suits your personal needs. The larger the C2 value the lower the audio-output level during transmit.

C1 is a miniature transistor-radio tuning capacitor. It is adjusted for maximum signal response at the receive frequency. You may substitute a trimmer capacitor for the panel-mounted variable capacitor, then peak the signal response for the center of any narrow frequency range in the 80-meter band.

The VBFO, Q4, has no buffer stage to provide isolation. Therefore, there will be some interaction between the local-oscillator frequency and the adjustment of C1. If you don't object to adding some low-cost circuit elements, you may add a 2N3904 or 2N2222 as a VBFO buffer. Injection to gate 2 of Q1, in either event, should be between 4 and 6 volts pk-pk.

Transmitter: A two-stage transmitter is represented by Q5 and Q6 of Fig. 4-3. C7 is the feedback capacitor. If you have difficulty making your crystal oscillate, experiment with the value of C7 until fast oscillator starting takes place. Values between 100 and 1000 pF are typical for 80-meter operation.

T2 is a narrow-band, tuned transformer. It provides an approximate impedance match between Q5 and Q6. Output from Q6 is filterby a 5-element low-pass network. D4 acts as a protective clamping diode to limit positive collector-voltage peaks to 36. This prevents damage to the 2N3866 if a mismatch occurs. You may use other transistors at Q6, such as the MPS-U02, 2N2102 and a host of other devices that have similar dc ratings. The fT should be at least 10 times the operating frequency.

D2 and D3 limit the signal level to the receiver during transmit, thereby protecting Q1. The 0.1-uF bypass capacitor at J3 may be increased in value for the purpose of shaping the CW note.

A VFO may be used ahead of Q5 by removing the crystal (Y1) and installing a 0.1-uF capacitor at C7. The VFO should deliver between 2 and 3 volts RMS to the base of Q5 [Z(base) approx. equal to 500 ohms]. If a VFO is used, it will have to be muted or shifted in frequency during receive periods.

Since the Gutless Wonder represents a suitable mainframe for later experimenting, you will probably think of many refinements that aren't mentioned here.

Parts List for Fig. 4-3

C1 -- Miniature 365-pF receiving variable.
C2 --See text.
C5 -- Miniature 75-pF air variable.
C6 -- 100-pF mica or ceramic trimmer.
D1 -- 9.1-V, 400-mW Zener.
D4 -- 36-V, 1-W Zener.
L1 -- 7-uH inductor. 38 turns of no. 26 enam. wire on an Amidon
    T68-6 toroid core (yellow).
L2, L3 -- 1.77-uH inductor. 19 turns of no. 24 enam. wire on
    an Amidon T50-2 toroid core (red).
R1 -- Audio-taper, carbon-composition, panel-mount control.
RFC1 -- Miniature 22-uH RF choke.
RFC2 -- 15 turns of no. 26 enam. wire on Amidon FT-37-43 toroid.
T1 -- 44 turns of no. 28 enam. wire on Amidon T68-2 toroid core.
    Link has 6 turns of no. 24 enam. wire. Secondary winding is
    12 uH.
T2 -- 14-uH primary. 50 turns of no. 30 enam. wire on Amidon
    T68-2 toroid. Secondary has 10 turns of no. 26 enam. wire.
Y1 -- Fundamental crystal, 30-pF load capacitance.

4.3 Chapter Summary

There are countless published circuits that cover the transceiver
and trans-receiver motifs. Many of these circuits may be found
in the material referenced in the final chapter of this book.
Your enthusiasm and ingenuity will make it possible to modify
the circuits shown here for other bands of operation. A recommended procedure is to first build the circuit as shown in this book,
get each stage to percolate properly, then modify one stage at
a time (and test it) for a different operating frequency. This
form of experimenting has long been a way of life for us radio
amateurs.

Your silent partner for circuit design and application is the
ARRL HANDBOOK. You will find the League's book, **Solid State Design
for the Radio Amateur** another valuable reference for this type
of work.

CHAPTER 5

THE QRP WORKSHOP

We may ask, "Why might a QRP workshop be different than any other Amateur Radio shop?" Perhaps the proper answer is, "QRP gear is smaller than QRO equipment." Therefore, large benches and heavy tools aren't required." But, there is more to be considered: Owing to the nature of QRP apparatus, the end product is usually lightweight and compact. This means that we may use a variety of low-cost cabinets and boxes for housing our circuits. The final product may look very "commercial," or we may settle for a completed assembly that has what some call a "hammy" appearance. My QRP friend and colleague, W7ZOI, refers to the latter technique as "ugly construction." There is an advantage to ugly construction: One can not only save money in the process, but will enjoy the advantage of fast assembly. This makes it possible to test and evaluate a new circuit quickly, and if circuit changes should be necessary (and they usually are!), we need not be concerned about messing up a "wholesome" looking module or chassis.

5.1 PC Boards

It is not difficult to lay out and etch our own PC boards. Some amateurs shy away from this part of home-style fabrication in order to avoid the mess that they think accompanies the use of etching solutions. Others feel that it is beyond their ability to lay out a PC pattern. Neither of these reasons is valid. If you can write your name, you should be able to lay out a PC pattern.

I start by drawing the circuit. Next, I collect the parts for the circuit. Step three calls for sketching the PC layout with a pencil on Quadrille paper (laid out with blue squares). This type of paper helps to ensure straight lines during the artwork exercise. I like to start at the beginning of a circuit, such as the crystal oscillator, first audio stage, etc., then work my way to the output port of the circuit. In my case, this calls for commencing the layout at the left side of the paper.

I try to predetermine the size of the PC board before drawing the circuit pattern. The boundries for the board are inked in to serve as fences or boundries that I must stay within. The PC pattern is then drawn as viewed from the etched-foil side

side of the board. This calls for being aware of the mirror-image syndrome; using care to avoid incorrect pin connections for trans-istors and ICs. You must always keep in mind that such components are being viewed from their <u>bottom</u> <u>sides</u>.

The next step is the laying out of one stage at a time. The proper spacing between PC-board holes can be determined by laying the significant component on the grid paper to learn where the mount-ing holes should be. Draw a circle for each of those points. The connecting lines between the circles may be drawn to a line width of approximately 1/8 inch (mm = 25.4 x inches).

Try to provide, early on, some lines that will serve as the +V and ground conductors, the full length of the PC board. This will make it easier to route the various circuit branches to the common power-supply feed lines. Most of my PC boards have a continuous copper border (about 1/4-inch wide) around the outer edges of the board. This serves as a ground bus to which circuit grounds may be run during layout.

Upon completing the rough pattern sketch, double check the pattern against the diagram to ensure that you have no errors, and that you have provided a place for each component. It is helpful to assign a part number (C1, R1, T1, etc.) to each circuit element. As you draw the pattern, mark the sketch to show where the parts belong. I use a red, green, blue and black pen for this purpose. That way if some parts-ID lines must cross, the various ink colors indicate exactly where the part belongs. Check all part numbers on the diagram against those on the pencil sketch. This will reveal whether or not you have left anything out.

The next task is to cut a piece of PC board to the size of your scale sketch. Clean the copper with steel wool. Next, place a piece of carbon paper over the PC-board copper. Tape it in place for a tight fit. Now, lay your sketch on the carbon paper, making sure the borders are aligned with those of the PC board, then tape the pattern in place. Use a ball-point pen to trace the pattern onto the copper foil, via the carbon-paper transfer. Remove the pattern and carbon paper. You may now use an artist's brush to apply etch-resist paint, or enamel household paint, to the pattern that is to be retained. Alternatively, you may use PC-layout donut pads and line tape to provide etch-resist protection for the copper elements. Press them firmly in place.

If paint is used as etch-resist, allow ample time for it to become dry. The etching solution may be ferric chloride or amonium per-sulphate. The ferric chloride is my preference, but it can leave stains the color of grasshopper spittle. *Always use plastic gloves when handling etching chemicals, and never breathe the fumes.*

Try to maintain the etching solution at 90 to 100 degrees F during the etching operation. Cold chemicals will result in poor etching over a long period. The warm solution should provide complete removal of the unwanted copper within 20 minutes, depending upon the thickness of the copper.

The PC board being etched should lie face down in the solution, and it should be agitated frequently during the process. This will wash away the copper residue to allow the etchant to reach the copper. The completed board should be rinsed thoroughly in clear, warm water, then dried with a paper towel.

The etch-resist paint may now be removed by rubbing it with a coarse grade of steel wool. If layout pads and tapes were used, they must now be removed from the PC board with a thin knife blade or hobby knife.

You may now drill the component holes in the board. Use a no. 59 or 60 drill bit for standard pigtail diameters. Some parts will require a slightly larger hole size, such as 1-W resistors, crystal sockets, trimmers, etc.

A little practice with the foregoing procedure will enable you to make your own one-shot PC boards with confidence. It is great fun to lay out a PC pattern -- much like working a puzzle. The finished product need not look like a work of art. It will work just fine, even if you think it is an ugly duckling!

5-2 Other Circuit Boards

We may avoid the etching exercise by using perforated circuit board (perfboard), which has no copper foil. Insert-type flea clips may be installed on the perf board for use as component tie points. You may use bus wire to join the appropriate flea clips.

Fig. 5-1C and D show alternative methods for making a circuit board. Illustration C shows how we may take a piece of copper-clad circuit board and cut square, isolated pads in the copper. A hacksaw is used for this purpose. A Moto Tool with a fine router bit may also be used to form isolated pads.

Fig. 5-1D shows how we may cut rectangular or square pads from a piece of circuit board, then glue them to a foundation of our choice, such as Formica, metal or another piece of circuit board. Hot-melt glue will get the job done quickly, or you can use 5-minute epoxy cement to affix the pads. The related pads may be joined with bus wire. Terminal strips, seen at the right in Fig. 5-1D, may be substituted for the isolated pads by soldering them to a piece of copper-clad circuit board.

5.3 Chassis and Enclosures

We need not pay the high price for boxes and cabinets when building QRP gear. Many ordinary household items can be utilized for
our projects. Take for example the illustration of a homemade
enclosure in Fig. 5-1A. Here we have an ordinary metal food can
that has been converted to an equipment cabinet. A panel end
plate has been cut from aluminum stock (such as a cookie tin).
The circular panel may be cut by means of a saber saw or nibbling
tool. A U-shaped chassis is formed from aluminum stock, then
bolted to the front panel as shown. The lip at the rear of the
chassis is used, by means of no. 6 sheet-metal screws, to secure
the chassis to the rear end of the can. Side brackets can be
formed, as shown, to keep the assembly upright during use. The
brackets may be attached by sheet-metal screws or no. 40 screws
and nuts. If sheet steel, such as furnace ducting, is used for
the panel and side brackets, you may solder the brackets to the
can, rather than using screws. Wood-grain contact paper or paint
can be applied to the can and brackets to impart a professional
look to the finished product. The appearance of the front panel
can be enhanced also by gluing a circular piece of Formica to
the metal panel.

Fig. 5-1B shows a method for using a flat sardine can as a chassis
base. L-shaped metal brackets are attached on the ends of the
can near the open end. A PC board may now be cut to match the
size of the opening, then you may attach it to the brackets by
way of sheet-metal screws. The various jacks and controls can
be mounted on the side walls of the can. A stroll through your
favorite food store will reveal all manner of containers that
are suitable for ham-radio projects. Don't overlook the many
foundation units that are available in the cookware department
of a variety store. Small, metal filing boxes (such as for recipe
cards) make ideal cabinets. Another container that offers many
possibilities for QRP equipment is the Band Aid box. The lid
may serve as a foot to elevate the equipment when it is in use.
A rubber band strung over the box (long way) will keep the cover
in place when it is used as a bail or foot.

Panel lettering can take the form of Dymo tape labels, press-
on decals, or letters typed on colored paper, then glued to the
panel. Ugly-look lettering may be applied by means of a laundry-
marking pen with a fine point.

5.4 Working with Toroids

It is best to think of coils wound on toroids as inductors that
contain a magnetic core, as is true of slug-tuned coils, filter
chokes, transformers and loop antennas with ferrite rods as cores.
The effect of the core material is to increase the inductance

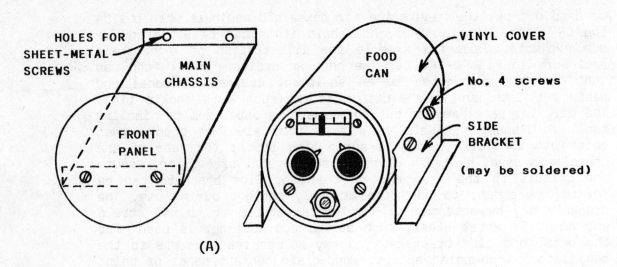

(A)

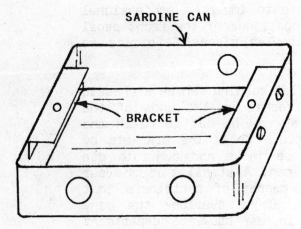

(B)

PRINTED-CIRCUIT BOARD

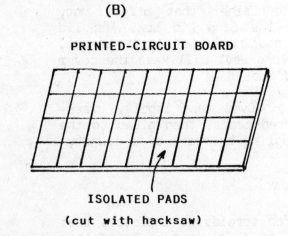

ISOLATED PADS

(cut with hacksaw)

(C)

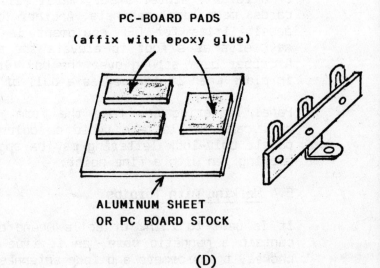

(D)

Fig. 5-1

of the coil, which means that fewer turns will be needed than when using an air-wound coil of equivalent inductance. One advantage of using suitable core material is that the winding resistance will be lower, owing to the use of larger wire diameters and fewer turns. This raises the Q of the coil over that of an air-wound coil with many turns of small wire.

Use the Proper Core Material: Ferrite and powdered-iron toroid cores are designed for specific operating frequencies. The Amidon Associates catalog lists the various cores versus recommended operating frequencies. The higher the core permeability, the lower the recommended operating frequency, respective to Q. Therefore, if you pick the wrong core for a job, the coil Q may be so low that the circuit will not perform properly. For this reason you should avoid buying bargain cores that bear no identification as to what the core recipe is. The same is true when buying surplus slug-tuned coil forms.

Ferrite cores have greater permeability, for a given size, than do powdered-iron cores. But, ferrite cores saturate more readily, for a given size (cross-sectional area) than is characteristic of powdered-iron cores. Saturation causes the generation of harmonic currents, causes core heating and possible permanent damage to the core, if it is a ferrite unit. Powdered-iron cores, on the other hand, will recover from overheating.

The flux-density rating of core material indicates how much power a core can accommodate before saturation commences. The formula is based on the cross-sectional area, the number of turns and the peak voltage in the winding. Data on these calculations is provided in equation form in the **ARRL Handbook** and my Prentice-Hall book, **Ferromagnetic Core Design & Application Handbook.** Both publications show an assortment of circuits for broadband transformers with various impedance-transformation ratios.

Generally speaking, powdered-iron cores are preferred for MF and HF amateur circuits. I use the no. 2 cores for frequencies up to 10.1 MHz. These are red-coded cores. The same color is used to identify the slugs in coils. Yellow cores (no. 6 material) are used from 10.1 through 50 MHz in my work. Various VHF cores are available for use above 50 MHz. This discussion is based on narrow-band applications, where the inductor or transformer is tuned to a specific operating frequency.

I use ferrite cores for narrow-band work at the lower end of the HF range. There is a frequent need for inductances of, say, 20 uH, which would require many turns of small wire if a powdered-iron core were used. The high permeability of ferrite results in a workable number of turns with larger wire. I use no. 61 material up to 10.1 MHz (125 permeability). From 10.1 to 30

MHz, I use no. 63 ferrite (permeability = 40). I do not employ ferrite materials above 30 MHz, except for broadband-transformer applications.

Ferrite cores are best for audio applications because of their high permeability. My choice below 1 MHz is no. 72 mix, which has a permeability of 2000. A 75 mix may also be used if greater permeability is required (5000 ui).

Toroidal inductors are self-shielding. This means that we do not need to enclose a tuned circuit in an electrical shield can in order to isolate one circuit from another. It does, however, create a problem: It is next to impossible to use a dip meter for learning the resonant frequency of a toroid and capacitor combination. The solution is to wind a temporary one- or two-turn link through the toroid, then connect it to a similar external link. The dip-meter probe coil may then be inserted in the external link to obtain a reading.

Broadband Transformers: There are two types of broadband transformer. One is known as a conventional transformer. The windings are arranged in the same manner as power transformers and RF transformers. The remaining type is known as a transmission-line transformer. It provides specific integers of impedance transformation, such as 1:1, 4:1, 9:1 and 16:1. Multifilar windings (two or more wires wound on the core at the same time) are used, and the phasing of the windings must be kept in mind when connecting the transformer to a circuit.

At the low end of the transformer operating range, the core increases the winding inductance. As the operating frequency is raised, the core effectively vanishes as a circuit element. Eventually, at the upper end of the operating range, it is as though only the winding remains. This accounts for the broadband characteristic of the component. Broadband transformers may be wound on ferrite rods, toroids or pot cores. The same is true of narrow-band transformers and inductors. Each core is rated for a specific AL factor, depending on the size and core material. The AL factor relates to the amount of inductance for a given number of turns. Knowledge of the AL permits us to calculate the number of turns needed for a specified inductance. The formula is 100 times the square root of the desired inductance, divided by the AL factor. Thus, if we needed 5 uH of inductance, and the core AL was 55, the number of turns would be 30. The Amidon catalog has a chart that tells the maximum number of turns versus wire gauge for various core diameters.

Circuit performance is the same whether a toroid, slug-tuned or air-wound coil is used in a tuned circuit. That is, there is no real difference between a fixed capacitor and slug-tuned coil than when using a toroidal coil and variable capacitor.

CHAPTER 6

QRP OPERATING

The QRP operating technique differs considerably from the procedure we may follow when using high power (QRO). In some QRO circles it is commonplace to stomp over the competition and hope to come out on top of the pile. We can equate this brutal form of operating to the child's game known as "King of the Mountain." The irony is that FCC regulations clearly state that the amateur shall use only the amount of power necessary to maintain communications. This precludes running a kW or more to talk across town! The QRPer, on the other hand, must rely on operating skill, timing and patience to get the same job done at the low-power level. We automatically become better operators because of the way we must operate in order to succeed in the crowded ham bands.

Some Simple Rules: (1) Don't expect answers when you call a very weak station. Chances are that he is running QRO, and by way of reciprocity your signal will be much weaker than his. He may not hear your signal at all! Try to answer stations that are Q5 and moderately loud. (2) Choose a clear frequency when calling "CQ." Spend some time listening on and near the frequency before "putting the fire to the wire." (3) Call CQ properly. Avoid long strings of "CQ" before giving your call sign. The other station is more interested in learning your call sign than listening to endless CQing. For example, "CQ CQ CQ de KA1BUQ, CQ CQ CQ de KA1BUQ, KA1BUQ K." (4) Use an effective antenna that is resonant and high above ground whenever possible. Avoid random-length wires and antennas that are low to the ground. Match the feed impedance to the transmission line (2:1 SWR or better). This will keep power losses at a minimum. (5) Keep your CW signal chirpless and free of hum. Do not use heavy "weighting" if you employ an electronic keyer. Too much weighting makes CW hard to copy, especially at the higher baud rates.

How Far Can I Work with QRP? DXCC is entirely possible with less than 5 watts of output power on CW. Under ideal conditions (bolstered by a good antenna) you should be able to work nearly everything you hear on 40 meters and higher. For example, I worked 42 countries in a 3-month period on 40 meters while running 1.5 W of RF power output into a full-wave loop antenna 35 feet high. As 8P6EU, VP2MFW, VP2VGT, ZF1ST, W1FB/VP2A and W1FB/KP2 I worked the world with rigs that provided 1.5 to 8 watts of output power. The antennas were sloping dipoles near the seashore. I generated many massive pileups and received numerous RST 599 reports.

6.1 Some Thoughts from QRP Societies

Although the ARRL is not a QRP society, it does embrace the QRP concept. The following words were written for use in this book.

> *97.67 (b) . . . amateur stations shall use the minimum amount of transmitter power necessary to carry out the desired communication.*

How often is this adhered to? Granted, there are times when QRO meets the above criterion. But more often, QRO results in wasting many kilowatt-hours of energy. In contrast, the QRP movement has been at the vanguard of meeting the above FCC directive.

The American Radio Relay League's operating program to promote QRP operation is best exemplified by the largest operating activity in the world -- namely, Field Day. This emergency field exercise has encouraged QRP operation for some 50 years. Today, if you want to "win," the scoring advantage gained from QRP operation overcomes the greater number of contacts made with QRO. For several years the ARRL International DX Contest has recognized QRP with a separate category, complete with certificates and plaques. And the prestigious Worked All States (WAS) certificate has long recognized QRP with a special endorsement sticker. In all such QRP operating achievements, the universally accepted definition of 10 watts input (or 5 watts measured output) is used.

The League also recognized that it is neither the sole nor necessarily the best agent for advocacy of specialty interests. In the promotion of QRP, the activities of QRP International are both well recognized and admired.

The future continues to bring us new technology. As we stand on the brink of a revolution in the use of digital techniques, radio amateurs may for the very first time truly be able to meet the letter of regulation 97.67 (b). The widespread use of "go-no-go" techniques, such as AMTOR, will permit the <u>lowest</u> threshold of power to effect communication. Thus, the cause of QRP may be enhanced beyond all imagination. It's exciting to speculate that QRP may prove to be the road into the future of Amateur Radio communications.

A sincere "73" to all who carry the QRP torch into the 21st Century.

John Lindholm, W1XX
ARRL Membership Communications Services
225 Main Street
Newington, CT 06111 (203) 666-1541

If you aren't an ARRL member, please consider joining the League. Your support of the official voice of Amateur Radio will strengthen the League's ability to protect our amateur frequencies through action in Washington, DC. The ARRL carries the battle flag in other areas of concern to radio amateurs, such as zoning-ordinance problems, emergency communications, etc. As a member you will receive **QST** each month, which frequently contains QRP circuits.

Some Words from QRP International:

Six words express the philosophy of this organization: Power is no substitute for skill.

Guided by that motto and the dedication of its members, QRP Amateur Radio Club International, Inc. has become the largest organization of low-power enthusiasts worldwide. Its members subscribe to the idea of running the least power necessary for effective communications. They can enjoy the hobby while lessening the impact on our already-crowded amateur bands. This overcrowding is often complicated by too many stations using too much power.

QRP ARCI was founded in 1961 by Harry Blomquist, K6JSS. It has no minimum or maximum power level to ensure that its members remain in good standing. But the club endorses and requires that its members follow the internationally recognized QRP power output levels of 5 watts (CW) and 10 watts (PEP SSB) for all of its contests, awards and other operating events.

In addition to these QRP levels, the club gives recognition to QRPp power input level of 5 watts or less (CW). It is one watt or less output for milliwatt (mW) operation. Not all organizations agree with the latter definition.

*QRP ARCI sponsors a full compliment of regional and national nets on a weekly basis. A net roster appears in each issue of the club bulletin, **The QRP Quarterly**, giving days of the week, times and frequencies, as well as the call signs of control stations. Nets are informal roundtables, open to all stations, regardless of affiliation or transmitter power. Check-ins count toward special certificates. These are part of the club's wide-ranging awards program, which is open to all low-power enthusiasts.*

QRP ARCI offers traditional types of awards. They are similar to those given by the ARRL (WAS, WAC, DXCC, etc.). It has a basic certificate for working 25 fellow club members, with endorsements for 50, 100 and upward.

***QRP Quarterly** is available for a free exchange of ideas about all aspects of QRP. Emphasis is on homemade gear. Full details about the club are available if you send an s.a.s.e. with postage for two ounces (or IRCs).*

QRP ARCI is dedicated to promoting and protecting the interests of QRP operators.

Vy 73,
Fred Bonavita, W5QJM
QRP ARCI
P.O. Box 12072
Capitol Station
Austin, TX 78711 USA

I would be remiss in my obligations to you if I did not include some words from our overseas QRP organization, the G QRP Club. Here are some comments offered for use in this book:

Dear Fellow QRPers:

I am happy and proud to write a letter to be included in the book on QRP by Doug, W1FB. For many years QRPers in the UK have had a high regard for Doug's work. **Solid State Design for the Radio Amateur**, of which he is a joint author, has become the standard work for all of us.

In the UK, QRP interests are closely linked with the building ·of one's own equipment. Most G-QRPers run stations which are completely or partly built by themselves. In Europe, QRP stations may be found on CW around 3560, 7030, 14,060, 21,060 and 28,060 kHz. The increase in interest in this facet of our hobby has been truly amazing. When I formed the G-QRP Club in 1974 I thought that our membership might just extend from the original 30 people to about 100. At the beginning of 1981 we enrolled our 1,000th member, and at the start of 1983 we were approaching 2,000.

We exist to promote the interest and growth in low power (5 watts or less) communication, and encourage the building and operation of one's own equipment. Our chief vehicle is a quarterly journal, **SPRAT**, which contains QRP views and news, and always features at least 2/3 practical circuits. If you are interested in our work, write to me and I will send you a sample of **SPRAT** and information about our club.

On behalf of the G QRPers, may I wish you pleasure on the bands, and success in your constructional projects.

Hpe CU QRP and 73,
Revd. George Dobbs, G3RJV
17 Aspen Drive
Chelmsley Wood, Birmingham, B37 7QX
UNITED KINGDOM

As the author of this book I wish to express my gratitude to John Lindholm, Fred Bonavita and Revd. George Dobbs for sending their thoughts and philosophies about QRP. This book would not be complete without their letters. I encourage each of you to consider becoming a member of the three societies represented by the foregoing QRP operators. The three official journals contain the kinds of information you will need to stay abreast of our QRP pastime.

The following is a current list of QRP operating frequencies provided to me in October of 1985 by Fred Bonavita, W5QJM:

CW	SSB	NOVICE
1810 kHz	?	0
3560 kHz	3985 kHz	3710 kHz
7040 kHz*	7285 kHz	7110 kHz
10,106 kHz	0	0
14,060 kHz	14,285 kHz	0
21,060 kHz	21,385 kHz	0
24,900 kHz**	24,950 kHz**	0
28,060 kHz	28,885 kHz	28,110 kHz
50,060 kHz	50,885 kHz	0

* G-QRP and some European clubs recognize 7030 kHz.

** These are tentatively designated 12-meter QRP frequencies at this writing.

Another QRP club that has a bulletin is the Michigan QRP Club. Its journal is called **The Five Watter**, and it is published quarterly. If you're interested in this club, contact the editor:

Mr. Thomas Root, WB8UUJ
538 Leland Street
Flushing, MI 48433 USA

APPENDIX A

This section of the book will deal with references that you will find useful in your quest for knowledge about QRP circuits. Additional data is offered concerning sources of supply for components that you will need when building QRP equipment. I can not testify to the integrity, speed of services or quality of the merchandise of the suppliers listed here. I have dealt with each of them on various occasions, and I have never had a problem. Caveat Emptor!

Recommended Books for All Amateurs

P. Hawker, G3VA, **Amateur Radio Techniques**, RSGB publication, available from ARRL, Inc. or RSGB, UK.

The ARRL Handbook for the Radio Amateur, ARRL, Inc., 225 Main St., Newington, CT 06111 USA.

D. DeMaw, W1FB, **Ferromagnetic Core Design & Application Handbook**, Prentice-Hall, Inc., Englewood Cliffs, NJ. Also available from Amidon Assoc., Inc. (see parts supplier list).

G-QRP Handbook, G-QRP Club, UK. See letter in chapter 6.

D. DeMaw, W1FB, **Practical RF Design Manual**, Prentice-Hall, Inc., Englewood Cliffs, NJ.

W. Hayward, W7ZOI, and D. DeMaw, W1FB, **Solid State Design for the Radio Amateur**, ARRL, Inc., Newington, CT 06111.

A. Weiss, WØRSP, **The Joy of QRP**, Milliwatt Books, Vermillion, SD 57069 USA.

Suppliers of Small Parts by Mail

A&A Engineering (W6UCM), circuit boards and QRP kits. 7970 Orchid Drive, Buena Park, CA 90620 (714) 521-4160.

Amidon Assoc., Inc., Bill Amidon, 12033 Otsego St., N. Hollywood, CA 91607. Catalog of toroids, pot cores and rods.

BCD Electro, P.O. Box 119, Richardson, TX 75080-0020 USA. (214) 238-0040 Surplus small parts -- catalog.

Circuit Board Specialists (WAØUZO), P.O. Box 969, Pueblo, CO 81002, circuit boards and QRP parts kits -- catalog.

Fair Radio Sales, P.O. Box 1105, 1016 E. Eureka St., Lima, OH 45802, (419) 223-2196. War surplus units and parts -- catalog.

Marlin P. Jones & Assoc., P.O. Box 12685, Lake Park, FL 33403-0685, (305) 848-8236. Small surplus parts and units -- catalog.

RadioKit, Box 411, Greenville, NH 03048, (603) 878-1033. New parts and kits.

State Street Sales (Dave DeMaw, KA1BUQ), P.O. Box 249, Luther, MI 49656. New surplus parts at low prices for QRPers and experimenters -- flyer for s.a.s.e.

ALL Electronics Corp., 905 S. Vermont Ave., P.O. Box 20406, Los Angeles, CA 90006 (1-800) 826-5432 --small parts and assemblies, catalog.

Suggested Magazine Articles

Receiving:

Hayward and Lawson, "A Progressive Communications Receiver," **QST** for Nov., 1981.

DeMaw, "Build a Bare-Bones Superhet," **QST** for June 1982.

Rusgrove, "Herring-Aid Five Receiver," **QST** for July 1976.

DeMaw, "Mini-Miser's Dream Receiver," **QST** for Sept. 1976.

Chadwick and DeMaw, "Receiving with Plessey ICs," **QST** for April 1981.

Rusgrove, "20-Meter High-Performance DC Receiver," **QST** for April 1978.

Hayward, "Unified Approach to the Design of Crystal Ladder Filters," **QST** for May 1982.

Transmitting:

DeMaw, "An Experimental VMOS Transmitter," **QST** for May 1979.

Lewallen, "An Optimized QRP Transceiver," **QST** for Aug. 1980.

DeMaw and Shriner, "Beginner's Three-Band VFO," **QST** for Jan. 1980.

Rusgrove, "A 20-Meter VXO, 6-W Transmitter," **QST** for Dec. 1978.

DeMaw, "Build this Sardine Sender," **QST** for Oct. 1978.

DeMaw, "Go Class B or C with Power MOSFETS," **QST** for Mar. 1983.

DeMaw, "Putting the 8P6 Special on 10 MHz," **QST** for Apr. 1983.

DeMaw and Martinek, "QRP Shakedown, Caymanian Style," **QST** for Mar. 1975.

DeMaw, "The 8P6 Special -- Hamcation Backup Rig," **QST** for Nov. 1982.

Hayward and Hayward, "The Ugly Weekender," **QST** for Aug. 1981.

DeMaw, "TR Circuits for Homemade Rigs," **QST** for Oct. 1984.

Other Articles for QRPers:

DeMaw, "Learning to Work with Toroids," **QST** for Mar. 1984.

DeMaw, "Magnetic Cores, A Second Look," **QST** for June 1984.

DeMaw, "Solar Electric Power and the Amateur," **QST** for Aug. 1977.

Note: Back issues of **QST**, when available, can be purchased from the ARRL. Photocopies of specific articles may be had from the ARRL for a nominal fee.

Ham Radio, CQ and **73** magazines have also carried articles on QRP gear over the years. Since I have no file of these publications, article referencing was not possible. A letter to these publishers may yield an index of QRP articles.

APPENDIX B

This appendix contains reference data that pertains to standard component values of interest to all build- ers of amateur equipment. The listings enable you to know what is available commercially in resistor, capac- itor, RF choke and diode values. This information is usually obscure, which requires digging through parts catalogs and brochures to find design values for your circuits. Additional component values are available for special resistors and capacitors, but these list- ings cover the popular values that you should be able to obtain easily.

Ceramic, Silver-Mica and Polystyrene Capacitors (picofarads)

3.3, 5, 6, 6.8, 8, 10, 12, 15, 18, 20, 22, 24, 25, 27, 30, 33, 39, 47, 50, 56, 68, 75, 82, 100, 120, 130, 150, 180, 200, 220, 240, 250, 270, 300, 330, 360, 390, 400, 470, 500, 510, 560, 600, 680, 750, 820, 910, 1000, 1200, 1500, 1800, 2000, 2200, 2500, 2700, 3000, 3300, 3900, 4700, 5000, 5600, 6800, 8200, 10,000

Electrolytic Capacitors [microfarads (uF)]

1, 2.2, 3.3, 4.7, 10, 22, 33, 47, 100, 220, 330, 470, 1000, 2200, 3300

Tantalum Capacitors (uF)

1, 1.2, 2.0, 3.3, 4.0, 4.7, 6.0, 6.8, 10, 15, 22, 30, 33, 47, 60, 68, 78, 80, 100, 120, 150, 180, 200, 220, 300, 330, 450, 470

Ceramic Trimmer Capacitors (pF range)

1.8-6, 2-8, 2.5-11, 3.5-20, 5.5-18, 5-30, 5-45, 5-55, 6-70, 7-25, 7-50, 8-25, 8-50, 9-35, 9-50, 12-70, 12-100, 15-60, 16-100

Not all of the above ranges are available from a given manufacturer. The numbers represent values that are listed by two manufacturers (Erie and Mouser). Many of the above values are found in low-cost plastic trimmers as well.

Computer-Grade Electrolytic Capacitors (uF)

550, 1000, 1200, 1400, 1500, 2100, 2200, 2600, 3900, 4500, 4600, 5600, 6200, 7600, 7700, 8000, 9600, 10,000, 11,000, 12,000, 13,000, 14,000, 15,000, 16,000, 17,000, 18,000, 20,000, 21,000, 23,000, 27,000, 30,000, 32,000, 34,000, 37,000, 42,000, 46,000, 47,000, 51,000, 63,000, 84,000, 88,000, 99,000, 100,000, 140,000

The above values represent those that are available from Mallory Corp. The voltage ranges for these capacitors run from 7.5 to 100, and not all capacitor values are available for each working-voltage value. Large-value capacitors (up to 2400 uF) are available by Mallory for use at 450 V (type CGS).

Resistors (carbon-composition) Standard Nominal Values

All values are in ohms. Bold face = 10% tol. Others are 5% units.
1.0, 1.1, **1.2**, 1.3, **1.5**, 1.6, **1.8**, 2.0, **2.2**, 2.4, **2.7**, 3.0, **3.3**, 3.6, **3.9**, 4.3, **4.7**, 5.1, **5.6**, 6.2, **6.8**, 7.5, **8.2**, 9.1, **10**, 11, **12**, 13, **15**, 16, **18**, 20, **22**, 24, **27**, 30, **33**, 36, **39**, 43, **47**, 51, **56**, 62, **68**, 75, **82**, 91, **100**, 110, **120**, 130, **150**, 160, **180**, 200, **220**, 240, **270**, 300, **330**, 360, **390**, 430, **470**, 510, **560**, 620, **680**, 750, **820**, 910, **1K**, 1.1K, **1.2K**, 1.3K, **1.5K**, 1.6K, **1.8K**, 2K, **2.2K**, 2.4K, **2.7K**, 3K, **3.3K**, 3.6K, **3.9K**, 4.3K, **4.7K**, 5.1K, **5.6K**, 6.2K, **6.8K**, 7.5K, **8.2K**, 9.1K, **10K**, 11K, **12K**, 13K, **15K**, 16K, **18K**, 20K, **22K**, 24K, **27K**, 30K, **33K**, 36K, **39K**, 43K, **47K**, 51K, **56K**, 62K, **68K**, 75K, **82K**, 91K, **100K**, 110K, **120K**, 130K, **150K**, 160K, **180K**, 200K, **220K**

Carbon Composition Resistors, con't.

The following values are in megohms. Bold-face numbers are for 10% tolerance. Other values are 5% tolerance.

0.24, **0.27**, 0.30, **0.33**, 0.36, **0.38**, 0.43, **0.47**, 0 51, **0.56**, 0.62, **0.68**, 0.75, **0.82**, 0.91, **1.0**, 1.1, **1.2**, 1.3, **1.5**, 1.6, **1.8**, 2.0, **2.2**, 2.4, **2.7**, 3.0, **3.3**, 3.6, **3.9**, 4.3, **4.7**, 5.1, **5.6**, 6.2, **6.8**, 7.5, **8.2**, 9.1, **10**, 11, **12**, 13, **15**, 16, **18**, 20, **22**

Carbon-composition resistors of the foregoing values are available in 1/8, 1/4, 1/2, 1 and 2-W values.

Zener-Diode Voltage Regulators

The following diode voltages (as listed by Motorola, Inc.) are available in 250-mW, 400-mW, 500-mW and 1-W units. Note: 1-W diodes start at 3.3 V; 250-mW diodes stop at 100 V; 400-mW diodes stop at 33 V.

1.8, 2.0, 2.2, 2.4, 2.7, 3.0, 3.3, 3.6, 3.9, 4.3, 4.7, 5.1, 5.6, 6.2, 6.8, 7.5, 8.2, 8.7, 9.1, 10, 11, 12, 13, 14, 15, 16, 17, 18, 19, 20, 22, 24, 25, 27, 28, 30, 33, 36, 39, 43, 47, 51, 56, 60, 62, 68, 75, 82, 100, 110, 120, 130, 140, 150, 200.

Toroidal-Core Information: Amidon Assoc., Inc. has specific codes for identifying its toroid cores. The ferrite units have an **FT** prefix, which means "ferrite toroid." The number that follows the prefix denotes the core diameter in inches. The last two number indicates the core mix (permeability is related to this). For example, an FT50-61 core is ferrite, 0.5-inch diameter, with an initial permeability (ui) of 125.

Powdered-iron toroid cores are identified as **T** (toroid) in the prefix. Next comes the size code, and the last numeral tells us the core mix (relating to permeability). Thus, if we had a T68-6 toroid core, it would be made of powdered iron, 0.68 diameter (inches), and the no. 6 suffix would indicate a permeability of 8. The following charts will be useful in selecting toroid cores for specific applications. Pot cores, rods and the slugs in variable coils follow the same general codes with regard to suffix numbers versus permeability. Most of the Amidon ferrites are manufactured by Fair-Rite Corp., and their powdered-iron toroids are made by Micrometals Corp.

Ferrite Core Mix	Permeability	Optimum Freq. Range Vs Q
63 mix	40	15 - 25 MHz
61 mix	125	0.2 - 10 MHz
43 mix	950	0.01 - 1 MHz
72 mix	2000	0.001 - 1 MHz
75 mix	5000	0.001 - 1 MHz

AL factors vary with the core diameter, thickness and mix. The Amidon Assoc. catalog lists the AL factors for the various cores.

Powdered-Iron Cores	Permeability	Optimum Freq. Vs Q
41 mix (green)	75	Audio to VLF
3 mix (grey)	35	0.05 - 0.5 MHz
15 mix (R&W)	25	0.1 - 2.0 MHz
1 mix (blue)	20	0.5 - 5.0 MHz
2 mix (red)	10	1.0 - 30 MHz
6 mix (yel.)	8	10 - 90 MHz
10 mix (blk.)	6	60 - 150 MHz
12 mix (gr/wh)	3	100 - 200 MHz
0 mix (tan)	1	150 - 300 MHz

AL factors vary with core diameter and thickness, plus permeability. See Amidon catalog for AL data.

Standard Nominal RF-Choke Values

It is helpful to know the available values for miniature RF chokes when designing QRP circuits. The uH and mH designations below are for solenoidal (single layer) chokes and single pi-winding chokes. Values listed for inductances greater than 100 uH are available in the single-pi format.

uH Values

1.0, 1.2, 1.5, 1.8, 2.2, 2.7, 3.3, 3.9, 4.7, 5.6, 6.8, 8.2, 10, 12, 15, 18, 22, 27, 33, 39, 47, 56, 68, 82, 100

Single-Pi (mH)

0.1, 0.12, 0.15, 0.18, 0.22, 0.27, 0.33, 0.39, 0.47, 0.56, 0.68, 0.82, 1.0, 1.2, 1.5, 1.8, 2.2, 2.7, 3.3, 3.9, 4.7, 5.6, 6.8, 8.2, 10

The above values are available in RF chokes manufactured by the J. W. Miller Co., Compton, CA. Low-cost miniature chokes of the above values (to 1 mH) are available from Mouser Electronics, Santee, CA.

INDEX

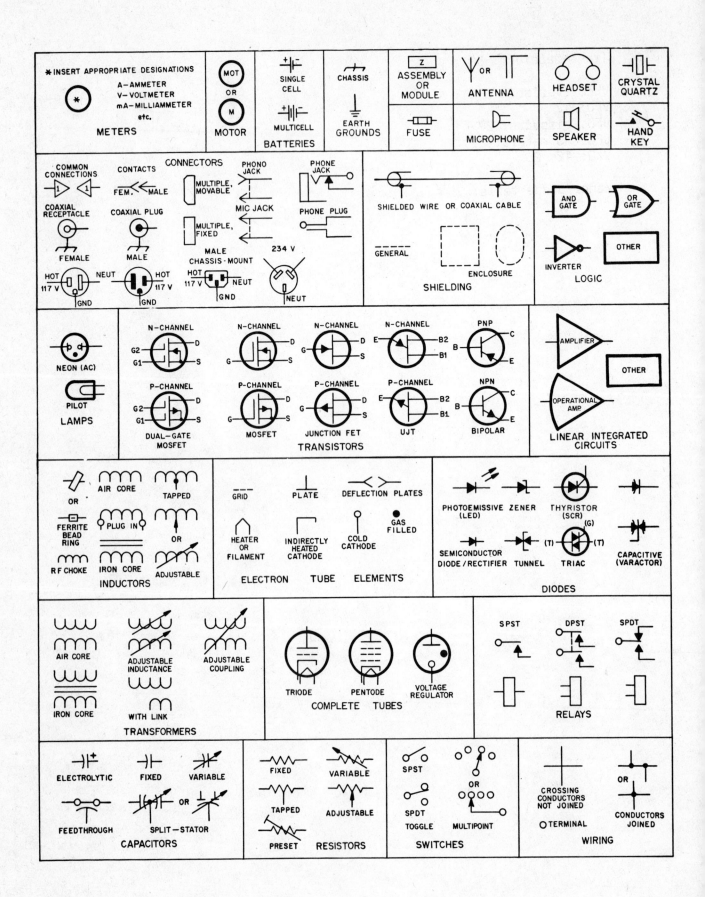

Please use this form to give us your comments on this book and what you'd like to see in future editions.

Name _____ Call sign _____

Address _____ Daytime Phone ( ) _____

City _____ State/Province _____ ZIP/Postal Code _____

From _____

_____

_____

Please affix
postage. Post
office will not
deliver without
sufficient postage

Editor, QRP Notebook
American Radio Relay League
225 Main Street
Newington, CT USA 06111

· · · · · · · · · · · · · please fold and tape · · · · · · · · · · · · ·